D0504781

TRACING YOUR FAMILY TREE

Stella Colwell

faber and faber
LONDON·BOSTON

First published in 1984
by Faber and Faber Limited
3 Queen Square London WC1N 3AU
Reprinted in 1984 and 1985
Photoset by Goodfellow & Egan, Cambridge
Printed in Great Britain by
Butler & Tanner Ltd, Frome and London
All rights reserved

Text © Stella Colwell, 1984

For my friends the family Clark—Ian, Elizabeth, Adrian and Maxwell—
and the family Garrett—Naame, Ken, Suzy and Stephen

British Library Cataloguing in Publication Data
Colwell, Stella
Tracing your family tree.
1. Great Britain——Genealogy
I. Title
929′.1′0941   CS414

ISBN 0–571–13246–4
ISBN 0–571–13590–0 Pbk

Contents

Illustrations

Acknowledgements

In the preparation of this book I have been given help cheerfully and generously by the following Grasmere people: Mrs Cathy Thompson, a descendant of the Greens, lent me photographs of her family; Michael Fearon, the Headmaster of Grasmere School, let me look at the school registers and logbooks; the late Frank Jarvis took photographs for me; the former and present Rectors of Grasmere, Dr Richard Bevan and Keith Wood, allowed me to root through parish records; and Brigadier Gordon Osmaston kindly helped to locate some of them.

To these and to all the Record Offices, Museums and Libraries which gave me permission to reproduce original documents in their care, I am immensely grateful, especially to the Archivist in Charge at Kendal, Sheila MacPherson, and the Librarian at the Wordsworth Library, the late Dr Peter Laver.

As for the text, I am solely responsible for it and any errors of fact are entirely mine.

The passage from Dorothy Wordsworth's letter of 28 March 1808 to Catherine Cookson, quoted on page 39, is taken from *The Letters of William and Dorothy Wordsworth*, volume 2 *The Middle Years*, 2nd edition 1969, edited by E. de Selincourt and revised by Mary Moorman, published by the Oxford University Press.

Transcripts of Crown copyright records in the Public Record Office appear by permission of the Controller of H.M. Stationery Office. The designs of the marriage, birth and death certificates in illustrations 4, 5, and 6 are Crown copyright and are reproduced with the permission of the controller of Her Majesty's Stationery Office, but Her Majesty's Stationery Office and the General Register Office accept no responsibility for any consequences whatsoever arising from the publication of parts of these certificates and typed extracts, and the responsibility is entirely the author's.

CHAPTER ONE
Tracing Your Family

EVERY FAMILY HAS a history.

The study of this history is called Genealogy, from the Greek words for 'race' and 'theory'. A family historian traces his genealogy back from himself to his earliest known ancestor, and to do this he searches for references to his family in old documents which may show a connexion between one generation and another.

You do not have to descend from a rich or famous family to be able to trace your ancestors. At least from the mid-sixteenth century almost everyone who ever lived in this country has been recorded somewhere. Knowing where to look and what to look for are what matters.

Sometimes, of course, the records may no longer exist or have been badly damaged so that they can no longer be read, or are not available to the public to search. This book is intended to signpost some of the roads you can follow to find your ancestors. Indeed, part of the interest is the research itself, working back from the known to the unknown, and the results can often be surprising. Because British society has always been very mobile you may discover ancestors from completely different social backgrounds. Do not be disappointed if your family tree reaches back only a few generations; you can still learn much about your ancestors' way of life, the world in which they lived and the local and national events of the period.

Each earlier generation traced introduces double the number of ancestors: you have two parents, four grandparents, eight great-grandparents, and so on. If you were able to trace all your ancestors over twenty-four generations, then you would have found 16,777,216 of them!

Some families intermarried with each other more than once, so that the number of actual ancestors is smaller than the potential total. Where two or more brides on

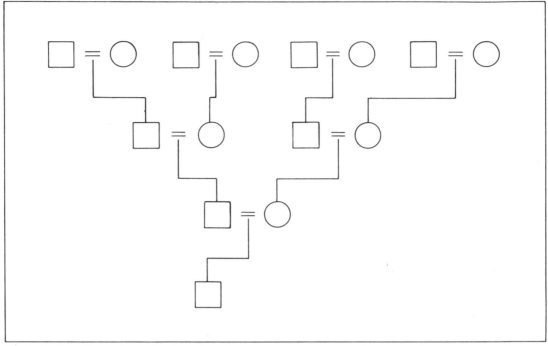

1 A simple pedigree chart, showing yourself, your parents, your grandparents and your great-grandparents. As you can see, the number of ancestors doubles with each generation. Male ancestors are shown as squares and females as circles

the family tree have the same surname you may well find that they had the same ancestry. However, the similarity of surname may be only a coincidence, especially if it was a common name, because not everyone of the same surname is related.

Surnames were originally used by individuals to distinguish themselves from their friends and neighbours, and died with them, but in time they became fixed and were used by a whole family. They were transmitted to the next generation, becoming hereditary. It did not happen at once, nor at the same time for all the families living in a particular area. In England hereditary surnames began to be used some time between the late thirteenth and mid-fifteenth centuries, depending on social class and where a family lived. Surnames generally derived from personal nicknames (Redhead, Little), occupations (Wheeler, Smith), dwelling places (Hill, Cornwall), or patronyms. An example of a patronym is Robertson: a man takes his father's Christian names, in this case Robert, and the suffix '-son', to make the surname. This originally changed with every generation.

In Wales, even until the nineteenth century in rural areas, a person was identified by a string of personal names. This was his family tree. Thus Llewellyn ap David ap Evan ap Richard was Llewellyn son of David son of Evan son of Richard. In Scotland

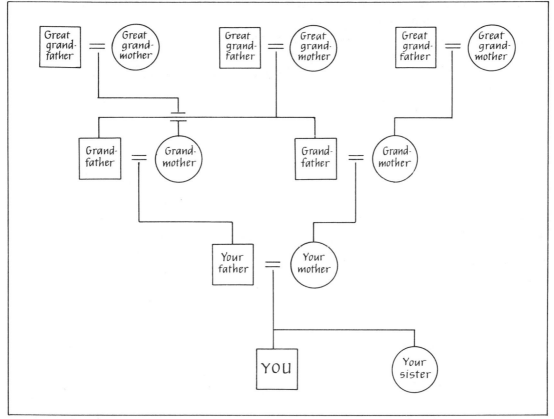

2   *This pedigree shows that when ancestors intermarry the number of forebears is smaller than in the simple pedigree chart. Here there are only 3 sets of great-grandparents instead of 4, because the two grandfathers were brothers. The father and mother were thus first cousins*

and Ireland the clan system was firmly established. The descendants of the founder of the tribe, his 'children' or clan, used his forename with the prefix Mac-, or O'. Thus the MacDonalds all descend originally from a man called Donald, and the O'Neills from Neill.

The family historian normally traces his ancestry in the male line. This is because the surname remains the same in each generation. It is best to tackle only one side of your family's history at a time, to avoid confusion. If you get stuck with your paternal ancestry, then you can turn to your mother's or grandmothers' families, tracing them through the male line too.

HAS IT BEEN DONE BEFORE?

The first step is to find out if anyone has traced your family's history already. I have

17

listed five books which you will find useful in the book list at the end of this chapter. However, these relate only to family trees in print. Even if your pedigree has been printed it may contain elements of guesswork or wishful thinking, so you should use it only as a guide for your own researches.

Perhaps a relative has prepared a family tree, or knows of someone else who has. It is a good idea to ask.

TOOLS OF THE TRADE

Essential tools for the efficient family historian are a notebook, loose-leaf file paper and a ring-binder, a pencil and rubber, a map of the area where the family lived, and a large sheet of paper on which to plot out the family tree in pictorial form.

A notebook should be used at all times to jot down what you have found and where, and ideas for further searches. Your findings can later be transferred on to the file paper and placed in the ring-binder. If you have time to write carefully you can copy down the information directly on to the file-paper, but if you are working at speed with dirty documents a clean sheet can end up as an illegible scrawl. It is safer to make notes and write them up later.

File-paper should be of a standard size, with a margin for notes. Use a separate sheet for each document examined. They can be filed in the binder according to generation, with the latest generation at the front, or according to the type of source you have consulted with the latest date at the bottom. You can rearrange the sheets as searches progress. Always head each sheet with a description of the type of document you have searched, where you read it, and its reference number if it had one. Did you look at an original document or was it printed in a book? If the record you consulted covered a period of years, what period did you search? Did you note down all entries of your surname and its variants, or only those relating directly to your family? What variant surnames did you note down? Make sure that you looked at both sides of a document; sometimes information was added on the back at a later date. Ensure that you have found the date of the document, and that you have written down all the essential details from it.

Always spell the names exactly as you see them. If you have difficulty in reading a word, look down the page to see if it occurs somewhere else where it may be more clearly written. You may be able to read the rest of the sentence and work out what the word should be. If not, then try finding the individual letters elsewhere on the page and build up the word gradually. If this fails, then copy down the word exactly as it appears. By getting the feel of each letter as it is written you can sometimes identify a word. If not, then you can try to decipher it later with a fresh eye, and isolated from the words around it in the original script.

Even if a search has been a complete failure you should still note what records you examined in the way described above. This will save needless duplication of searches.

Record Offices often require you to use a pencil when making notes, because many of the documents you will see are unique and fragile. Pencil notes are also easier to correct and erase.

The pedigree chart setting out your family tree and the map of the area where they lived should be constantly used for reference, so that you can quickly see what point you have reached and in which places to start looking next. A map will indicate not only place-names but roads and landscape features, and distances between settlements. An Ordnance Survey map of 1/50000 should be sufficient. If you need a more detailed map Record Offices usually have a good collection of large-scale maps of the area.

TALKING TO RELATIVES

Jot down in your notebook a list of those living relatives whose names you know, and write the address of each person against his name. Then draw up a list of questions to ask them about themselves, their children, and their forebears.

Here is a sample of the sort of information you should aim to collect, allowing a separate page for each relative interviewed:

1. Date of interview
2. Full name of person interviewed
3. Address at the time of interview
4. Occupation or profession at that time
5. Any different occupation previously?
6. Why was the occupation changed, and when?
7. Date and place of birth
8. Date and place of marriage
9. Full name of husband/wife
10. Full names of any children, with the date and place of birth written alongside each
11. Religious denomination
12. Father's full name
13. Father's residence now, and his occupation
14. Mother's full name and surname before marriage
15. Date and place of parents' marriage
16. Date and place of father's birth
17. Date and place of father's death and burial
18. Date and place of mother's birth

19. Full names of her parents
20. Date and place of mother's death and burial
21. Names and addresses of aunts and uncles
22. Full names of grandparents.

If you arrange your visit well in advance, it will give your relatives time to collect together family documents and heirlooms, which may contain very useful clues about names and events.

Some answers will be less complete than others, or will contradict what you have been told by someone else in the family. Memories are often defective, and people will only tell you what they wish you to know, so try to talk to as many members of the family as possible to build up the picture.

Coax your relatives to recount stories from their childhood and write them down. These tales can give you some idea of what games they played, the sort of schools they went to and the friends they made; of their first jobs and how far they had to travel to find work, and what they were paid; of members of the family long since dead, where and how they lived.

COLLECTEANA

Perhaps they have kept family papers and oddments, such as old diaries, letters, postcards, photographs, wedding invitations, birth announcements, In-Memoriam cards, birth, marriage and death certificates, old passports, Army call-up papers, newspaper cuttings, scrapbooks, prizes, badges from uniforms, a Family Bible, an embroidered sampler or other handiwork.

If you are allowed to see these, examine them carefully and list the various items with the date when seen, and where and who was the present owner. Make copies of them if possible; at least note the names, dates and places of everyone named in them. If you are lucky enough to trace a Family Bible, this may include details of the wedding of the couple to whom it was given, with the names of all their children added as they were born, and their dates of birth.

Photographs and newspaper cuttings can be tantalizing because they are often unnamed and undated. Try to fill in these gaps when you talk with your relatives, and label the items on the back, or ensure that your notes about them include this information. Ask if you can obtain copies of the photographs, not only of the people but of the houses where they lived. Besides being a historical record of the family their portraits over several generations can show what they looked like and how they dressed.

DRAFTING A PEDIGREE

By now you should have accumulated a vast array of information, and you will need

JACK LOAN

3　My father's effects: birth certificate, 11 November 1903, World War II Defence Medal, pouch containing USA Alien Seaman's Identification Card, World War II ration book, 3 blood transfusion badges, Boy Scouts' Thanks badge, Observer Corps badge, Pendant watch, chain and tobacco tin, Photographs showing him as a young man in the uniform of the British Mercantile Navy, in the uniform of the Observer Corps and in his garden at Grasmere, Observer Corps arm badges, British Mercantile Marine button, Scouts Annual, 1923, The Boys Own Annual to organize it in a pictorial way. You will require a very large sheet of lined or blank paper (about 1m×700cm; a piece of lining wallpaper would do, but be careful not to tear it). It is best folded up when not in use, as a roll is inclined to be bulky to carry around and gets frayed and untidy-looking at the edges.

Write your own name about three inches up from the bottom, and then allow about two inches above this before adding the names of your parents. Allow similar space for every previous generation. If your father has any brothers and sisters, then write their names on the same line as his, in order of birth, the oldest on the far left and the youngest on the far right. If you want to include husbands and wives, then the wife's name should be written on the right of her husband's. Any children of your aunts and uncles should be written on the same line as yourself, because you are all in the same generation. By displaying each person in the same generation on the same line you can easily identify them and their relationship to other members of the family. Draw a horizontal line connecting the names of the children of the same parentage, and finally draw a vertical descent line joining them up to their parents.

Here is a check-list of the facts you should aim to include on the pedigree, in the order I should recommend.

1. Full name
2. Present address
3. Occupation
4. Date and place of birth
5. Where educated and any University degree
6. Date and place of death and/or burial
7. Date of his will and when it was proved
8. Under the names of females only, the date and place of marriage follows 5.

In this way you have prepared an outline family history. Before you embark on searches of public records, it is wise to show the pedigree chart to each of the relatives who helped you with information in case they can add anything more.

If you have no surviving elderly relatives, try to visit the cemeteries or church-yards where they are buried and note down full details of any gravestone inscriptions to the family. The information in them can be as useful as a starting-point as that given by living relatives.

Book List
G.K.S. Hamilton-Edwards   *In Search of Ancestry* 1976
G.K.S. Hamilton-Edwards   *In Search of Scottish Ancestry* 1972
Heraldic Artists Ltd   *Handbook on Irish Genealogy* 1980
P.H. Reaney   *A Dictionary of British Surnames* 1958

P.H. Reaney   *The Origin of English Surnames* 1967
G.W. Barrow   *The Genealogist's Guide* 1977
G.W. Marshall   *The Genealogist's Guide* 1903, 1967
J.B. Whitmore   *A Genealogical Guide* 1953
T.R. Thomson   *A Catalogue of British Family Histories* 1976
M. Stuart and J. Balfour Paul   *Scottish Family History* 1930
J. Unett   *Making a Pedigree* 1971

CHAPTER TWO
Family Records: the Colwells

FOR THIS INTRODUCTORY tour of the records family historians find most useful I have chosen the pedigrees of the Colwells, the Greens, and the Wordsworths to illustrate the types of information you can glean from old documents. The Colwells are my own family, and I have selected the other two because of their connexion with Grasmere, the Lake District village where I grew up. The poet William Wordsworth lived with his family at Grasmere between 1799 and 1813. In 1808 he wrote a poem about two villagers, George and Sarah Green, who perished in a blizzard in March that year. When I went to Grasmere School two of George's and Sarah's descendants were among the pupils.

I shall describe the family history of the Greens in Chapters 4–7, and that of the Wordsworths in Chapter 8. In this chapter and the next I shall explain how I discovered some of the history of my own family.

When I began my research I had very little to go on by way of background information. I had heard from my father that his paternal grandfather farmed at Simonside, County Durham. My father is dead now, but his two younger sisters remember that their grandfather and his wife retired to a house in Laburnum Terrace, East Boldon, County Durham, where both died while my aunts were children. The house in Laburnum Terrace passed to my grandfather, William James Colwell, and he lived there with his wife and three children until about 1926, when they moved to Glasgow. During the First World War he served in the Royal Armoured Service Corps in Mesopotamia (now Iraq), and he brought back a small fragment of inscribed clay from the wall of King Nebuchadnezzar's palace as a souvenir. After the move to Glasgow he was a buyer of goods for a firm of gentlemen's outfitters.

My grandfather died in 1947, when I was only three, so I remember very little about him. I wanted to know when he was born, and to discover this I had to find out how old he was when he died.

RECORDS OF BIRTHS, ADOPTIONS, MARRIAGES AND DEATHS

Since 1st July 1837 copies of all registered births and deaths, and of marriages of all religious denominations and those which took place in Register Offices, in England and Wales, have been kept centrally. These records are held at the General Register Office in London, together with Adoption records dating from 1927. The indices to the records are open to the public from Monday to Friday, between 8.30 a.m. and 4.30 p.m., but you have to pay a fee in order to obtain certified copies of the entries in the registers.

In Scotland central registration did not start until 1st January 1855, and the records are held in Edinburgh, where you can look at them yourself on payment of a search fee. These too are indexed.

In Ireland all births, marriages and deaths registered since 1st January 1864 are recorded in Dublin, though marriages between Protestants had begun to be registered from 1st April 1845. Since 1st January 1922, when southern Ireland became an independent republic and Northern Ireland remained part of the United Kingdom, Northern Irish records have been housed in Belfast. I have listed the addresses of all these repositories at the end of this book.

All these registers have separate indices of births, of marriages and of deaths. The indices in the General Register Office in London are arranged in four yearly volumes, one for each quarter. Thus a birth registered in February would be found in the index covering the period between January and March.

The death indices run alphabetically by surname, and then by Christian name, followed by registration district and number, and the page reference to the entry on the register. From March 1866 until June 1969 the indices state age at death; after this the date of birth, when known, is given instead. Having found the entry you require you must then complete an application form for a death certificate, copying out the details from the index, and take it to the desk. Having paid for your certificate in advance, you are given a receipt. Normally it will take about two days for the certificate to be ready for collection, and you must hand over your receipt to collect it. Certificates can be sent by post, but this takes longer.

The death certificate will tell you the date and place of death, the name, sex, age and occupation of the deceased, the cause of death, and the name and address of the person who informed the local Registrar of the death, with his relationship to the dead person. The informant was either a witness of the death or had been present in the same house at the time.

The death indices for 1947 gave my grandfather's age as fifty-six. He must have been born in or about 1891 according to this, possibly in County Durham where his parents were said to have farmed. Unfortunately none of the four indices covering 1891 contained his name. I widened the search to take in the years around it, starting with 1890 and 1892. Finally I found him in the index for the September quarter of 1880, ten years earlier than I had expected. The index showed his surname, Christian names, birth registration district and number, and page reference to the register. If he had been born after July 1911 the index would also have included his mother's surname before marriage.

William James Colwell's birth certificate revealed that his parents were William Colwell and Elizabeth his wife, formerly Gibson. His mother registered the birth, which took place at home.

4   *The marriage certificate of William Colwell and Elizabeth Gibson, my great-grandparents, dated 1877*

Now I was able to start looking for the marriage entry of the above couple in the marriage indices. I had to check both surnames to make sure that the details of registration district and number, and the page reference tallied. To make the task easier I looked under the more unusual surname, that of Colwell. From March 1912 the indices give a cross-reference to the surname of the other spouse against each entry, which makes searching easier.

It is a good idea to search a period of at least fifteen years back from the birth of the first known child, and a few years afterwards as well. In this case the marriage was found three years before the birth of William James, in the June quarter of 1877. The marriage certificate told me that the bride and groom lived in the same street, and that Michael Colwell, the groom's father, was then dead. Matthew Gibson was one of the witnesses, and he was probably a relative of the bride. Using the clue of

CERTIFIED COPY OF AN ENTRY OF BIRTH   GIVEN AT THE GENERAL REGISTER OFFICE, LONDON.

Application Number 192 B.

			REGISTRATION DISTRICT		*Castle Ward*				
1841.	**BIRTH** in the Sub-district of		*Ponteland*		in the *County of Northumberland*				
Columns:—	1	2	3	4	5	6	7	8	9	10*
No.	When and where born	Name, if any	Sex	Name, and surname of father	Name, surname, and maiden surname of mother	Occupation of father	Signature, description and residence of informant	When registered	Signature of registrar	Name entered after registration
362	Twentieth of November 1841 Eland Hall Township of Ponteland	William	Boy	Michael Colwell	Ann Colwell formerly Hownam.	Farmer's Son	The mark of Ann x Colwell Mother. Eland Hall	Twenty ninth of December 1841	Proctor Registrar	—

5   *The birth certificate of William Colwell, dated 1841*

William Colwell's age, thirty-six, I was then able to search for his birth entry in the indices around 1841. He was born on 20th November 1841, at Eland Hall, Ponteland, Northumberland, to Michael Colwell, farmer's son, and Ann Colwell, formerly Hownam. A search of the marriage indices produced no entry under Hownam, but I did find an Ann Howman in the same registration district and number as Michael Colwell in the March quarter of 1840. When the marriage certificate was obtained I saw that her name was quite clearly written as Hownam. This shows that the clerks who compiled the indices sometimes made mistakes.

So by working back from my grandfather's death in 1947, I had succeeded in tracing my ancestry to the beginning of the period of central registration in 1837. You may not need to purchase as many certificates as I did if your family can give you more dates and names than I was able to collect.

WHAT TO LOOK OUT FOR
Occasionally you will fail to find an ancestor's name in the indices. This may be because of a clerical error like the one I found, or because your information about age or name was inaccurate. A nickname, or an extra Christian name added later, can cause confusion. Transposed or dropped Christian names are not uncommon: for example, Thomas Herbert was perhaps later called Herbert Thomas or Herbert only. Sometimes a child was registered under entirely different Christian names from those by which he was later known. If the name is changed at baptism, it appears on the certificate itself in the far right-hand side, but it does not appear in the index. An infant whose parents had not decided on its name might be registered merely as a 'male' or 'female' birth. These registrations are found at the end of each surname list.

There may be surname variants that you have not checked. When you are looking at the indices it is always a good idea to examine all possible variations of the surname you are searching for and to list them. This will avoid having to repeat the search.

Births had to be notified to the Registrar of the district where they took place, and within forty-two days of the birth. If the birth occurred in March, June, September or December, then it may have been registered too late for inclusion in the quarterly returns made during those months. You should therefore look in the following quarter as well.

Occasionally the local Registrar omitted entries when he made his quarterly returns to the Registrar General in London. If you know where a child was born, but cannot find his name in the central indices in London, write to the appropriate Registrar whose records cover that district. A check of the original registrations may well reveal the missing entry.

A birth certificate normally gives the mother's maiden surname. If she had been married before, sometimes her former married surname appears instead, yet when she remarried she had used her maiden surname. This makes searching difficult, but may account for a missing entry. In this case, if the groom's name is unusual, or the registration district is the same as that where the birth took place, you can have a check made of the marriage registers against her Christian name, and if it does not agree with your information then you will be given a refund of part of the fee.

Some families did not bother to register their children's births, although legally obliged to do so, and their names will be absent from the indices.

Adoption certificates do not contain details of actual parentage. A child's surname and personal names given to him on adoption, plus those of his adoptive parents, are completed by his date of birth and date and place of adoption. In certain circumstances you can apply to the Registrar General for further information concerning adoptions after 1927, but you must be at least eighteen years old.

Deaths had to be registered within five days, before burial. Ages on these certificates can be quite misleading, as in the case of my grandfather. This is because the informant of the death may have had to guess the age, or the deceased himself may have lied about it. If you use this age as a guide as to when to start looking for the birth certificate then you should allow a margin of ten years on either side of the approximate date of birth.

When you are consulting birth and death certificates, look at the name and address of the informant. My great-grandfather's death certificate, dated 1st August 1912, showed that he had another son, M.G. Colwell, living with him at Laburnam Terrace, East Boldon, about whom I previously knew nothing.

Marriage certificates may be inaccurate or incomplete. The ages of groom and bride are often unreliable, or are merely stated as 'full' or 'over twenty-one'. A person not of full age was described as a minor. A minor had to obtain parental consent to marry. If this was not forthcoming, sometimes the minor's real age was

CERTIFIED COPY OF AN ENTRY OF DEATH   Given at the GENERAL REGISTER OFFICE, LONDON.

Application Number _____ 203 H .

REGISTRATION DISTRICT				South Shields				
1912. DEATH in the Sub-district of South Shields					in the Counties of Durham &c			
Columns :— 1	2	3	4	5	6	7	8	9
No.	When and where died	Name and surname	Sex	Age	Occupation	Cause of death	Signature, description, and residence of informant	When registered	Signature of registrar
134	First August 1912 South Shields Workhouse Infirmary Harton South Shields	William Colwell	male	70 years	Of 3 Laburnum Terrace East Boldon formerly a Farm Labourer	1 Chronic Nephritis 2 Syncope Certified by D Spence MB	M G Colwell Son 3 Laburnum Terrace East Boldon	Fifth August 1912	James Sedcole Registrar

6   *The death certificate of William Colwell, dated 1912*

concealed by stating at his marriage that he was of full age. Where one party was much older than the other a few years might have been deducted or added on to make the difference less obvious.

When a marriage ended in divorce the records of the decree absolute were filed at Somerset House, London. They date from 1857 and you cannot search them nor the indices to them, but on payment of a small fee a search will be made for you. Until fairly recently divorce was an expensive business, so relatively few couples bothered to take the matter to the Courts.

RECORDS OUTSIDE ENGLAND AND WALES
Scottish certificates are much more informative than English ones. Birth certificates also contain the date and place of the parents' marriage, while death certificates supply the names of the parents and spouse of the deceased. Marriage certificates give the names of mothers as well as fathers of both parties.

Irish certificates follow the English model.

If your forebears worked abroad or came here from overseas, then you will find that records of their births, marriages and deaths vary between the Scottish and English certificates in the amount of detail they give. You can obtain the addresses of Registrars General overseas from the General Register Office in London. You may find that central registration began much later than it did in this country.

Records of British subjects who were born or died at sea on British vessels between 1837 and 1965 are held in the General Register Office in London, and are indexed as Marine Returns. Births, marriages and deaths of British subjects registered with the British Consulates abroad from 1849 until 1965 can also be searched for there. From 1966 onwards the returns of both of these are entered in one register, and you can consult the indices to them. The General Register Office also holds Regimental

Registers of births, marriages and deaths of Army personnel and their families between 1761 and 1924; registers of these events relating to all the three Armed Service Departments for the years between 1796 and 1965; returns of people killed in South Africa during the Boer War (1899–1902), during the First World War (1914-1921), and the Second World War (1939–1948); and births and deaths which occurred in civil aircraft from 1947 until 1965. Indices to all of these are on the open shelves of the General Register Office and the fee for a certificate is the same as for an English one.

As you can see, it is not just events which took place in England and Wales that are centrally registered, so if members of your family travelled abroad or served in the British Army, Royal Navy or Royal Air Force then you can easily check to see if their names appear in the above indices.

CHAPTER THREE
The Census: the Colwells

THE FIRST CENSUS, or overall population count, in the United Kingdom was made on the night of 10th March 1801, and a Census has been taken at ten-year intervals ever since, except in 1941, during the Second World War. The 1841 Census was the first to contain names. The Census Returns are a very important source of information for the family historian, because they reveal how and where people lived at the time, where they came from, and family relationships. They also record names of children who perhaps did not survive to adulthood. Most important, they tell us about the dates and places of birth of people born long before the period of central registration. Because of the way they are arranged it is possible to find a whole family group in the Census Returns, whereas when you are looking for birth, marriage and death certificates you are searching for individual people.

The Returns are organized by hamlet, village or township, and then by household. Specially appointed local officials, called Census Enumerators, went round the houses in their district delivering Census forms to the head of every household. The head completed the form giving details about all those people in his household on the night set aside for the Census count, and this was later collected by the Enumerators, who passed on all the forms to the local District Registrar of Births and Deaths. The Registrar copied up all the information from the forms into special books which were then sent to the Registrar General in London.

In the 1841 Census street and house names were rarely given. Nor was the relationship of the people in the house to the head, their marital status, nor their birthplace beyond whether it was in the county in which they were recorded in the Census, or elsewhere. Ages were rounded down to the nearest multiple of five, so that a person of sixty-seven would be described as sixty-five. Exact ages were given of children of fifteen and under.

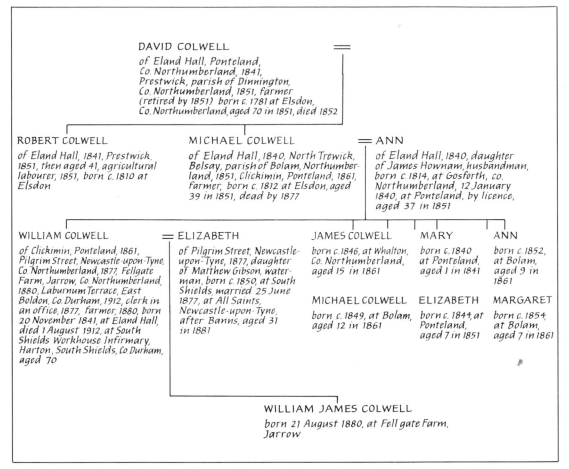

7   Four-generation pedigree of the Colwells, covering roughly a century, to 1880

The Census taken on the night of 30th March 1851 recorded house names or numbers, as well as streets, and there are typescript street indices for some of the larger towns and cities, pinpointing their exact place in the Returns. The Returns also give the relationship of every person in the house to the head, their marital status, age as notified by the head, rank, profession or occupation, and birthplace. They even indicate whether a person was blind, or deaf and dumb. This pattern was followed by the Census Returns of 7th April 1861, 2nd April 1871, and 3rd April 1881, with an additional column to indicate where a person was an imbecile, idiot or lunatic. There are street indices to the 1871 and 1881 Census Returns of the whole country to help you to locate a particular address.

By looking at a sequence of Census Returns you can learn how a family expanded or diminished in size, the names and number of its offspring, the names, ages and

Township of Ponteland

PLACE	HOUSES		NAMES of each Person who abode therein the preceding Night	AGE and SEX		PROFESSION, TRADE, EMPLOYMENT, or of INDEPENDENT MEANS.	Where Born	
	Uninhabited or building	Inhabited		Males	Females		Whether Born in same County	Whether Born in Scotland, Ireland, or Foreign Parts
Eland Hall		1	Jacob Gilkespy	55		Ag Lab	y	
			Mary Do		60		y	
			Margaret Do		11		y	
Do	1	1	Robert Elliot	60		Miller	y	
			Francis Do	20			y	
			Mary Do		15		y	
			Jane Do		12		y	
			Jane Do		11 months		y	
Do		1	David Colwell	60		Farmer	y	
			Robert Do	30			y	
			Michael Do	30			y	
			Ann Do		25		y	
			Mary Do		1		y	
			William Watson	20		Ag Lab	y	
			Anthony Potts	20		Ag Lab	y	
			Margaret Warde		20	F S	y	

8   An extract from the Ponteland census for 1841. Eland Hall was an estate containing a number of homesteads. Double slanting lines indicate separate buildings; a single slanting line indicates a separate household within the building. We can therefore see that David Colwell and his family shared a house with two agricultural labourers and a female servant, but that these three appear to have belonged to a separate household. HO 107/823 Crown copyright

No. of Schedule	Road, Street, &c., and No. or Name of House	HOUSES		Name and Surname of each Person	Relation to Head of Family	Condition
		In-habited	Unin-habited (U.), or Building (B.)			
1	Clickimin	1		Michael Colwell	Head	Mar
				Ann Do	Wife	Mar
				William Do	Son	Un
				Elizabeth Do	Daur	Un
				James Do	Son	Un
				Michael Do	Son	Un
				Ann Do	Daur	Un
				Margaret Do	Daur	Un

9 *An extract from the Ponteland census for 1861, showing the household of Michael Colwell, at Clickimin.*

birthplaces of elderly relatives lodging with them, and how occupations varied within the family and from one Census to another. You will also discover changes of address, the acreage of land farmed by the family, and the number of employees, apprentices and servants who worked for them.

The Censuses of 1841, 1851 and 1861 told me quite a lot about my own family. My great-grandfather William Colwell's birth certificate, dated 20th November 1841, told me where his parents were living at the time. This enabled me to find them in the Census Returns for that year, although William himself was born after the Census night of 7th June. I learned that David Colwell, my great-great-great-grandfather, was a farmer aged about sixty, living at Eland, Hall, Ponteland, Northumberland, with Robert Colwell, aged about thirty, Michael Colwell, also aged about thirty, Ann Colwell, aged about twenty-five, and Mary Colwell, one. They were all natives of Northumberland. Two agricultural labourers and a young servant girl were in the house, probably David's employees.

The 1851 Census records that David Colwell was by then aged seventy; he was a widower, and had retired from farming. He was living at Prestwick in the parish of Dinnington, close to Ponteland, and had two grandchildren staying the night, including William Colwell, aged nine, and an unmarried son of forty-one who, like himself, was born at Elsdon in Northumberland, about fifteen miles to the north west. My great-great-grandfather, Michael Colwell, was not found either in Ponteland or Prestwick, but from the 1861 Census Returns I learned that he had moved back to farm at Ponteland, on a holding of 153 acres at Clickimin, and

Age of		Rank, Profession, or Occupation	Where Born		Whether Blind, or Deaf and-Dumb
Males	Females				
49		farmer 153 acres 3 Labourers	Northumberland	Elsdon	
	47	Wife	Do	Gosforth	
19		Son	Do	Ponteland	
	17	Daur	Do	Do	
15		Son	Do	Whalton	
12		Scholar	Do	Bolam	
	9	Do	Do	Bolam	
	7	Do	Do	Do	

You can see from the map on page 37 that Clickimin lies next to Eland Hall. The different birthplaces of the children reflect the family's movements over the previous 19 years. RG9/38 52 Crown copyright

employed three labourers. Michael was born at Elsdon, and among his six children were two born nine and twelve years before at Bolam, a parish lying about eight miles north-north-west. Using this information as a clue, I was able to locate Michael and his family in the 1851 Census Returns of Bolam, living on a farm of 221 acres called North Trewick, and employing one man and a general servant.

By the time of the 1861 Census David Colwell's name had disappeared. A search of the death indices at the General Register Office in London revealed that he died in the March quarter of 1852. Looking at the 1841, 1851 and 1861 Census Returns I had learnt that David came from Elsdon and some time after 1812 he moved to farm at Ponteland. He was probably a widower by 1841. His son Michael left home either in 1841 or 1842 and took his family to Bolam. He returned to Ponteland between 1854 and 1861, but did not take over his father's farm. By 1871 the Colwells had left Ponteland, and Michael's son William was an office clerk living in Newcastle upon Tyne in 1880.

The Census also records population totals. From these I learnt that 424 people lived at Ponteland in 1841, and this total had increased to 488 by 1861. We know the acreage of Michael's farm from the 1861 Census, but we have to rely on a map made of the township around the time of the 1841 Census for the size of his father's farm, which ran to 228 acres. You can see from this map where David Colwell's farm, Eland Hall, lay in relation to Clickimin, their comparative shapes, and the situation of their farm buildings. From the information accompanying the map I found that David's landlord was Matthew Bell. Maps like this can add more to the picture given by the Census Returns and I shall say more about them in Chapter 6.

LANDOWNERS.	OCCUPIERS.	Numbers referring to the Plan.	NAME AND DESCRIPTION or LANDS AND PREMISES.	STATE or CULTIVATION.	QUANTITIES IN STATUTE MEASURE.			Amount of Rent-Charge several Lands, and to PAYABLE TO Vicar		
					A.	R.	P.	£.	s.	d.
Bates Joseph and Williamelsabl	Bates & Wm Atkinson	29	House & Garden at Ponteland		"	"	28	"	"	9½
Bates Elizabeth	Herself	14	House and Garden at Ponteland		"	"	25	"	"	9½
Bell Matthew Esquire	David Colwell	22	Eland hall farm		228	1	10	25	2	8

10   *The tithe apportionment of the township of Ponteland lists landowners alphabetically. From this we can see that David Colwell was a tenant farmer (plot No. 22), that his landlord was Matthew Bell, and that the farm extended over 228 acres, 1 rod and 10 perches. IR 29/25/362 Crown copyright*

HOW TO USE THE CENSUS RECORDS

The English and Welsh Returns are held at the Public Record Office in London, but only those over a hundred years old are available to the public; you can inspect the microfilmed copies of the Registrars' Books. You have to be aged ten or over before you can use the microfilms, and you will need a reader's ticket. You can obtain this, in the form of a day pass, on your visit to the Public Record Office. The Office is open between 9.30 a.m. and 4.50 p.m., Monday to Friday, and last orders for microfilms must be placed before 4.15 p.m. It may be useful to know that you do not have to come to London to see the Census microfilms. Many County Record Offices and libraries have purchased copies of local Returns; they are often less crowded than the Public Record Office and have more flexible opening hours. (See the book list at the end of this chapter.)

English and Welsh Census Returns for the years 1891 and 1901 are held by the Office of Population Censuses and Surveys, in London. On payment of a fee, a search can be made for you of a specific address, for a named person's age and birthplace. You must be a direct descendant of this person, or have the written consent of a direct descendant, or of the person himself if he is still alive.

Scottish Census Returns from 1841 have been deposited in New Register House, Edinburgh, and can be examined by the public up to 1891. Unfortunately, almost all the Irish Returns between 1861 and 1891 were destroyed by fire in 1922, although Returns survive from 1841 and 1851. You can inspect surviving Returns to 1911 at the Public Record Office in Dublin.

You must be prepared to find some of the Census Returns difficult to read, because the microfilms show up the lettering as white on a black background. If you cannot read a particular word such as a birthplace or a person's name, write it down exactly as it appears and analyse it later with the help of a Gazetteer, or the Returns of a subsequent or previous Census in which you found the family. The Census columns for ages are organized by males and females, so you can at least discover a person's sex if not his Christian name. If he was born after July 1837, you could try searching the birth indices at the General Register Office for an entry which tallies with the given year of birth and the registration district appropriate to his birthplace.

When you are looking at the Census it is a good idea to note down all other entries of the surname in a particular place. Even if you cannot find your direct forebear one of these people may have been his brother or sister, a parent or other relative, and their ages and birthplaces can give clues as to when and where to search next. Every household in a place should be investigated in case your ancestors were lodgers, guests, employees or apprentices in someone else's house. Elderly

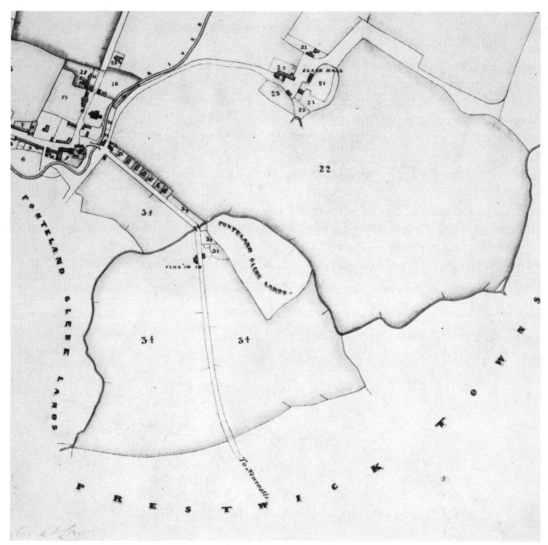

11   Having found David Colwell's name in the tithe apportionment you can find Eland Hall farm in this tithe map of the township of Ponteland, drafted on 17 April 1841. IR 30/25/362 Crown copyright

relatives staying in the household are a bonus for the family historian, because their ages and birthplaces not only take the family back a generation, but they point to where the family came from.

The relationship of members of the household to the head is given, not their relationship to the person whose name appears immediately above their own. Ages may be inaccurate, either because the head of the household did not know them exactly or deliberately added or knocked a few years off for his own reasons. Similarly, occupations were sometimes exaggerated to raise a person's social status, while some appear merely as initials. For example 'FWK' means 'framework knitter', and 'FS' and 'MS' mean that a person was a female servant, a farm servant, or a male servant. Birthplaces may be incorrectly given, but even so they may indicate where the family lived round about the time of the birth. 'NK' indicates that the birthplace was not known.

Having found the family you are looking for it is important always to take full, accurate copies of the Census entries. You should include the year when the Census was taken, the microfilm reference number, the town, village or hamlet concerned and its enumeration district number, folio and page references, plus the entry number, the house name or number and the name of the street. This means that if you want to read the entry again you can find it with the minimum of effort. If you have searched several places you should list them even if you found no reference to your surname, and your notes should also clearly record whether you looked merely for your direct ancestors or for any mentions of your name. This is so that you will know exactly what you have done if you need to repeat a search later.

Book List
J.S.W. Gibson   *Census Returns 1841, 1851, 1861, 1871 on Microfilm: A Directory of Local Holdings* 1979

CHAPTER FOUR
Parish Registers: the Greens

THE PARISH REGISTERS of Grasmere show that on '25 March 1808 were buried George and Sarah Green his wife of Blintern Gill, Grasmere, perished in a snowstorm on the Mountains between Grasmere and Langdale, in a dark tempestuous night'. On 28th March Dorothy Wordsworth wrote a letter to a friend from her home at Dove Cottage, Grasmere, telling what had happened: 'Most likely you have read in the papers of the dismal event which happened in our neighbourhood on Saturday . . . George and Sarah Green two inhabitants of this vale went to a sale in Langdale in the afternoon; and set off homewards in the evening, intending to cross the fells and descend just above their own cottage, a lonely dwelling in Easedale. They had left a daughter at home eleven years old, with the care of five brothers and sisters younger than herself, the youngest an infant at the breast. These dear helpless creatures sat up till 11 o'clock expecting their parents, and then went to bed thinking that they had stayed all night in Langdale because of the weather. All next day they continued to expect them, and on Monday morning one of the boys went to a house on the opposite side of the dale to borrow a cloak. On being asked for what purpose he replied that his sister was going to Langdale to lait their Folk who had never come home. The man of the house started up, and said that they were lost; and immediately spread the alarm. As long as daylight lasted on that day, and on Monday and till Tuesday afternoon, all the men of Grasmere and many from Langdale were out upon the Fells. On Tuesday afternoon the bodies were found miserably mangled, having been cut by the crags. They were lying not above a quarter of a mile above a house in Langdale where their shrieks had been distinctly heard by two different persons who supposed the shrieks came from some drunken people who had been at the sale. The bodies were brought home in a cart, and buried in one grave last Thursday.'

FRANK JARVIS

12   The Greens' cottage at Blintern Gill. The Langdale Valley lies beyond the hills in the background

Luckily, many of Dorothy Wordsworth's letters have been published, and by reading these and the Grasmere parish registers I was able to piece together the story of the Greens.

The baptism registers of Grasmere reveal that the eleven-year-old daughter left in charge of her younger siblings was Jane Green, christened on 16th October 1796, and that the baby was baptized Hannah on 4th January 1807. The four other children still at home were George, baptized on 23rd December 1798, John, baptized on 12th October 1800, William, baptized on 19th February 1804, and Thomas, who was baptized on 7th April 1805. At first the family lived at Kitty Crag, but some time between 1800 and 1804 they moved across the Easdale Valley to

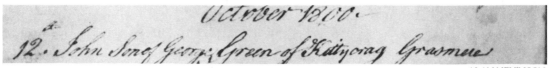

ALAN NEVINSON

13   The entry of John Green's baptism in the parish register of Grasmere. It reads: 'October 1800 – 12th – John son of George Green of Kittycrag Grasmere'

40

Blintern Gill. A search of the earlier parish registers revealed that George and Sarah Green had two older children baptized at Grasmere: Mary on 3rd November 1793, and Sarah on 8th February 1795. By 1808, according to Dorothy Wordsworth, Mary was in service at a local inn, and Sarah was nursemaid to the children of Dorothy Wordsworth's brother William at Dove Cottage.

FRANK JARVIS

14   Dove Cottage, Grasmere, where William and Dorothy Wordsworth lived from December 1799 to June 1808. Before they rented it, it was an inn called the Dove and Olive Bough

As George and Sarah Green had no children baptized before 1793 I looked at the Grasmere marriage registers and found that their wedding took place on 18th August 1792. George Green was a widower and Sarah's maiden name was given as Wilson. Both George and Sarah marked rather than signed the register, indicating that they were probably illiterate. When I searched the burial registers back from 1792 I

ALAN NEVINSON

15 *The marriage entry of George Green and Sarah Wilson in the Grasmere parish register, 12 August 1792. Both parties made their mark instead of signing the register*

discovered that George's first wife, Jennet, was buried on 23rd April 1786, a fortnight before their son George. Villagers told Dorothy Wordsworth that they had died of a malignant fever and no one had dared to approach the house for fear of infection. Grasmere baptism registers showed that George and Jennet had a family of two sons and three daughters christened between 1766 and 1777. From 1766 until at least 1768 they lived at Goody Bridge, lower down the Valley, and moved to Blintern Gill before 1771, where they still were at the time of Jennet's death in 1786. From the marriage registers I learned that George Green married Jennet Mackareth on 22nd September 1765. A that time he was a husbandman, while his bride was a servant. The two witnesses who signed the marriage register were John Green and George Mackereth [*sic*], probably relatives of the couple. George Green was baptized on 20th September 1741, the son of John Green of Guddy Bridge, and the parish registers contain references to Greens in Grasmere from the late sixteenth century.

When I was at Grasmere Elementary School two of my schoolmates were descendants of this George and Sarah Green. The grandfather of one of them was Felix Burns Green. Felix was baptized at Grasmere on 27th February 1895, having been born on 30th January, and his parents were James Green, a slate quarryman, and Sarah. He was their second child. James and Sarah did not marry at Grasmere Church, but the Superintendent Registrar's records at the Kendal District Registry show that they were married at the Independent Chapel of the Wesleyans, Ambleside, on 26th March 1890. James was then aged twenty-nine, a slate-river, living at Church Town, Grasmere, the son of Thomas Green, domestic gardener. The birth registrations record that James was born on 6th January 1861, at Loughrigg, in the parish of Grasmere, and that his mother's name was Mary Jane and her maiden name was Routledge. At the time of the 1861 Census James was three months old, and had an older brother called George, then aged one. The family resided at Clappersgate, on the outskirts of Ambleside. As neither child was baptized at Grasmere Church I looked at the parish registers of Ambleside and located George's baptism there on 12th June 1859, although no trace was found of James.

In 1861 their father, Thomas Green, was aged twenty-eight. He was born in Ambleside about 1833, while his wife came from Penrith in Cumberland, some thirty miles to the north. At the time they married at Grasmere Church on 20th November 1858, Thomas was a gardener living at Ambleside, and was described in the marriage register as the son of John Green, husbandman. The 1851 Census of Ambleside showed that Thomas was living with his parents on Chapel Hill. John Green, his father, was aged fifty, an agricultural servant, and a native of Grasmere, while his mother Jane was aged forty-five, and came from nearby Hawkshead, in Lancashire. Thomas and their three daughters were all born in Ambleside. Thomas was baptized at Ambleside Church on 13th May 1832 and was the couple's second child. Altogether six children were baptized there, and George, the eldest, was buried at Ambleside on 6th June 1837, aged seven. John Green married Jane Jackson at Grasmere on 20th June 1829. As John was fifty in 1851, he must have been born in 1800 or 1801. I looked at the Grasmere baptism registers and found that he was christened on 12th October 1800; he was the son of George and Sarah Green, the couple who died in the snow in 1808.

PARISH REGISTERS

Much of our information about the Green family comes from the parish registers of Grasmere. From 1538 every church in England and Wales was obliged to keep a register of all baptisms, marriages and burials in the parish. In Scotland these registers did not start to be kept until 1558, and in Ireland not until 1634. The registers were stored in a special parish chest. The registers are still used to record baptisms, marriages and burials in the churchyard, but many of the older ones have been deposited in County Record Offices. Some registers have been copied and printed, and can be consulted in the County Record Office, County Library, or at the Society of Genealogists in London. Others are still in the churches. The County Record Office can advise you as to the whereabouts of a parish register. In Scotland the parish registers are held at New Register House, in Edinburgh, and you can search them on payment of a fee. The Public Record Office in Dublin hold some parish registers, but many others stored there were consumed by fire in 1922. The rest are kept in the churches.

If the registers are at the church you should ask the Vicar or Rector for an appointment to search them. You can obtain his name and address from the current edition of Crockford's *Clerical Directory*, which covers Anglican clergy and their livings throughout the world. If you write to him, remember to enclose a stamped self-addressed envelope for your reply. A search fee will normally be charged, based on the time taken.

Few parish registers actually survive from 1538. Many were lost, destroyed by fire, damp or other mishap. The entries during the years 1645–1660 were often incomplete because of the Civil War, the establishment of a new system of government called the Commonwealth, and the replacement of the Anglican establishment by the Presbyterian as the State Church. During this period the parish registers passed into the custody of a special parish official, who was not always careful in the way he kept the records, and indeed sometimes failed to return the registers to the church after the Restoration of the Monarchy and the Anglican Church in 1660. The Institute of Heraldic and Genealogical Studies, at Canterbury has produced a useful series of maps of the English and Welsh counties, plotting out parish boundaries as they were in 1837, and including dates of the earliest known surviving parish registers for each place.

Up to 1753 all the baptisms, marriages and burials were written into the same register, but from 1754 a special book was used to record marriages. In 1813 baptisms began to be written into a special baptism register and burials were recorded in a burial register.

From 1813 baptisms were written in columns; there were columns for the date, baptismal names of each child, his surname, the full names of his parents, their place of residence, the father's occupation and the signature of the Minister who officiated at the ceremony. Before this, usually only the date, the child's names and those of his parents were given.

Burial registers from 1813 were also organized in columns. The details included were the date of the funeral, the full names, abode and age of the dead person, and the signature of the officiating Minister. These burial entries are useful in calculating approximate years of birth, as well as telling where a person lived. Prior to 1813 the burial registers normally only mention the date of burial, and the person's name.

BURIALS in the Parish of *Grasmere* in the County of *Westmorland* in the Year 1891				
Name.	Abode.	When buried.	Age.	By whom the Ceremony was performed.
Henry Robinson No. 1067.	Unknown a Tramp found Dead near Above Beck	February 26	54	Henry M. Fletcher
John Green No. 1069.	Grasmere	March 14	90	Henry M. Fletcher

ALAN NEVINSON

16   The burial entry of John Green, son of George and Sarah Green, in the Grasmere parish register, 14 March 1891. On the same page is recorded the burial of Henry Robinson, aged 54, 'a tramp found dead near Above Beck'

Some include a female's marital status, or a child's parentage, but they rarely give ages.

Between 1667 and 1814 bodies had by law to be buried in woollen shrouds. This was to try to revive the flagging woollen industry. Someone, usually a relative, had to swear on oath that the body had been wrapped in wool. The parish registers often record that the Affidavit was made.

Occasionally the initial letter 'P' was written against a burial entry. This indicates that the person was a pauper and the funeral was paid for out of parish funds. This fund was made up of money collected from parishioners and was known as the Poor Rate.

From 1754 to July 1837, all marriages had to take place in an Anglican church. Only Jews and Quakers were exempt, and they held their own ceremonies and kept their own marriage registers. The registers of Anglican marriages from 1754 contain the full names of groom and bride, their current marital status, parish of abode, and give the date of the wedding and whether it was after Banns or by Licence. Both parties signed the register, and at least two witnesses and the officiating Minister added their signatures. Marriages normally took place in the bride's church, but these registers give a clue as to where the groom came from. Before 1754 merely the date of the wedding and the names of the parties were recorded. If one party did not come from that parish then sometimes his place of abode was included. The initial letters 'o.t.p.' written against a name mean that he was 'of this parish', while 'b.o.t.p.' means that both parties were of this parish.

A bride often took her first child back to her home parish for baptism, so it is always worth having a look at the registers for a few years after the marriage. Later children were usually baptized where the couple made their own home. Sometimes it is worth looking at the baptism entries for a few years before the marriage: Sarah Wilson, George Green's second wife, had two illegitimate children baptized at Grasmere in 1789 and 1791.

Often you will find that your ancestors did not remain in the parish very long. The parish registers may give you a clue as to where they came from, but if not, then you will have to search the registers of the parishes nearest to it, casting the net further afield.

BANNS BOOKS AND MARRIAGE LICENCES

From 1754 all marriages took place after Banns or by Licence. Banns, or declared intentions to marry, were read out by the Minister during services on the three Sundays preceding the wedding day. They were read out in the churches of both parties, and details of them were written into a special Banns Book which was then kept in the parish chest. If you cannot find a particular marriage a look in the Banns Book may tell you the name of the parish where the other party lived and thus lead you to the church where they were married.

Some people preferred to buy a Licence to marry from the ecclesiastical authorities. Often they were wealthier folk, people who wanted the privacy of a Licence rather than the publicity of Banns, or who wanted to marry in a hurry, or who were not members of the Anglican Church and did not want to sit through a church service to listen to the Banns being read out. The applications for Marriage Licences, called allegations and bonds, contain information about the groom's and bride's places of abode, their current marital status, age and occupation, as well as the church in which they wanted to marry. If you cannot find a marriage a look at the indices or lists of Marriage Licences can at least tell you something about the distribution of the surname over a particular area and give you a clue as to which parishes to search next.

Basically the Bishop and his Archdeacons granted Licences for marriages of local people within the diocese and its archdeaconries, but sometimes Incumbents had the right to grant Licences for marriages in their own churches, and the Archbishops of York and Canterbury had overall control over licensing of marriages between

The *second* —— Day of *October* in the Year of our LORD One Thousand Eight Hundred and *two* #

ON which Day appeared perfonally *William Wordsworth of Grasmere in Westmoreland Gentleman*

and, being Sworn on the Holy Evangelifts, alledged and made Oath as follows, That he is of the Age of *Thirty two* —— Years, and upwards, and a *Bachelor* and intends to marry *Mary Hutchinson of Gallow Hill in the Parish of Brompton in the Diocese of York* Aged *Thirty* —— Years, and upwards, and a *Spinster*

—— —— —— ——

not knowing or believing any lawful let or impediment by Reafon of Confanguinity, Affinity, or any other Caufe whatfoever, to hinder the faid intended Marriage : And he prayed a Licence to Solemnize the faid Marriage in the *Parish Church of Brompton* —— aforefaid, in which faid *Parish* the faid *William Wordsworth* further made Oath, That *she* the faid *Mary Hutchinson* —— hath had *her* ufual abode for the Space of four Weeks laft paft,

On the fame Day the faid *William Wordsworth* was Sworn before Me

William Wordsworth

John Kirk

Surrogate

REPRODUCED FROM THE ORIGINAL IN THE BORTHWICK INSTITUTE OF HISTORICAL RESEARCH, YORK

17 *The marriage allegation of William Wordsworth, made on 2 October 1802 before John Kirk of the Vicar General's office of the Archbishop of York. Wordsworth and Mary Hutchinson were married at Brompton on 4 October*

people of different dioceses within their jurisdictions. It is a good idea to look at the records of all the authorities covering your area. Good series of records of licensing date from the late sixteenth century, although Marriage Licences were granted long before this. They are held in the Diocesan Registries or County Record Offices, and some have been printed. I have listed a helpful guide to Marriage Licences in the book list at the end of this chapter.

BISHOPS' TRANSCRIPTS

The problem for the family historian is the number of gaps which may occur in parish registers, or the total absence of entries before a certain date. From 1598 until the late nineteenth century every English and Welsh parish had to send to the Diocesan Registrar an annual copy of all baptisms, marriages and burials entered in the parish registers during the past year. These were called Bishops' Transcripts. Originally they were kept in the Diocesan Registries but nowadays many have been deposited in County Record Offices.

If the register has been lost or damaged for a certain period, these Transcripts may be the only means of discovering baptisms, marriages and burials. You should be careful to note down any gaps in the Transcripts, however, because some years may be missing from these as well. In the case of Grasmere there are Bishop's Transcripts from 1676 until 1877. There are longish gaps in the parish registers between 1583 and 1610, so that records of baptisms, marriages and burials during those years have been lost forever.

The Bishops' Transcripts were intended to duplicate the parish registers, so where the register is not available it may be more convenient to search the Transcripts. This is especially so if you want to look at a group of parishes whose registers have not all been deposited in the County Record Office, are not copied up and printed, or are defective for the period in question. You should, wherever possible, check the original registers as well, because the clerk who copied out the Transcript may have omitted or shortened entries for economy, or may have mixed up two entries to become one. Conversely, additions to and corrections of the parish register entries were sometimes made when the Transcript was written.

OTHER AIDS TO SEARCHING PARISH REGISTERS

Members of the American sect of the Mormons are particularly concerned, for religious reasons, with the details of their ancestors' lives, and they have collected a library of microfiches of birth, baptism and marriage entries taken from parish registers and other sources. Many County Record Offices are now buying copies of these. The microfiches are arranged by county and then alphabetically by surname, variants being grouped together. The Society of Genealogists in London has a complete set of updated microfiches for the whole country, and an Index of the places they cover and for what years. The microfiches, called the International Genealogical Index, can be a useful guide to the distribution of a surname in a county as well as being a source for finding births, baptisms and marriages of people out of their home areas. You should always inspect the original parish registers as well, because the microfiches are not infallible and may contain inaccuracies or miss some entries out altogether. You should not rely on them alone for your research.

Many parish registers have been copied and printed. The County Record Office should have a stock of local ones, while the Society of Genealogists has a very good collection arranged on county shelves with other local printed material. I have listed guides to original and printed parish registers in the book list at the end of this chapter.

A specially helpful series is Phillimore's printed marriage registers. Most of the English and Welsh counties are included, some more extensively than others. Generally both the registers and the Transcripts were consulted, and the period covered runs up to 1812, although some volumes go up to 1837. Like the marriage allegations Phillimore's printed marriage registers can produce isolated references to your family outside their home area, and show the distribution of a surname over a wide region. However, it is still a good idea to look at the original registers too, because the editors may have abbreviated entries, or made errors or omissions in copying and printing them.

Percival Boyd's Marriage Index, compiled between 1925 and 1956, covers many English counties. There is a complete copy of the typescript Index at the Society of Genealogists, and there is a printed handlist to the registers included by him and for what periods. The marriages were listed from parish registers and marriage allegations in print during the time he worked, so it is not fully comprehensive. The Index is divided into county volumes, and then into periods of twenty-five years from the late sixteenth century until 1837. Each county volume is indexed by surname, variants being grouped together, and there are separate volumes for males and for females, so that the entries cross-reference each other.

The Society of Genealogists also possesses a Great Card Index made up of slips recording over three million names with details of the original source in which they were found, its date, and other personal data. Sometimes a search can help trace a missing ancestor or give the distribution of the surname.

Lastly there is the Pallot Index of marriages, drawn largely from the registers of the City of London churches between 1780 and 1837, but also including entries from many surrounding parishes. The Index is not open to the public, but on payment of a fee a search can be made for you for a specific marriage or for all entries of a particular surname. The Index is held by the Institute of Heraldic and Genealogical

Studies at Canterbury, which has produced a typescript list of the parishes covered and for what periods.

USING THE REGISTERS

Although baptism was supposed to be within a fortnight of birth, often it was delayed by months or even years. Indeed, parents might wait until the family was complete and take them all for baptism on the one occasion. By the nineteenth century some families did not bother to have their offspring baptized at all, while others had abandoned the Established Church and become Dissenters, keeping their own records of birth and baptism.

You may find that two or more children born to the same parents were baptised by the same name. It was fairly common to give the name of a child who had died to a later infant, so look at the burial registers for the years in between the two baptisms for the older child. The first son of George Green of Blintern Gill was baptized George on 25th July 1768. This son was buried at Grasmere on 6th May 1786, and a later son, born after the second marriage, was also given the name of George at his baptism on 23rd December 1798. Some families deliberately christened two or more children by the same name even though the older one was still alive, because they wanted to make sure that a favourite or traditional name survived to the next generation. Another reason may be that one child was given the name of the Patron Saint on whose Festival Day he was born, while a later infant was given that of a godparent whose name happened to be the same.

Baptism registers should always be used in conjunction with the burial registers, especially as after 1813 dates of birth can be learned from the burials. From the burials you can also learn when various members of the family died, as infants, young adults or at an old age. Names absent from the burial registers suggest that these people had moved away from the district and were buried elsewhere.

A register may distinguish between two people of the same name by describing one as 'senior' and the other as 'junior', or as 'elder' and 'younger'. When these adjectives disappear you should search the burial registers to discover which one had died.

HANDWRITING AND DATING

As you trace your ancestors further back in time you will find that the style of handwriting changes too. Some letters will seem totally alien, while others will be written in different ways depending on the scribe. I have listed some books which you will find helpful in the book list at the end of this chapter.

Spelling was also a matter of personal habit until the late eighteenth century, so be careful to search all the variants of your surname and to spell them as they appear in the records. Some variants may not be obvious, as surnames were often spelt as they were pronounced in local dialect. While such words give you an idea as to how your name was pronounced they can often be confusing. For example, in Norfolk the surname of Tuddenham was written as Tudenham, Tudman and Studman in one parish register.

Until 1752 New Year's Day was 25th March in England and Wales. Written records before this show baptisms, marriages and burials under the old calendar. Thus, a child baptised on 22nd March 1731 would have been baptised on 22nd March 1732 by our modern reckoning. It is important to leave the dates as you see them when noting down references to your family, and to modernize them later, as you may remember to alter some dates as you go along, and not others, and end up with a jumble of useless information. From 1st January 1752, however, New Year's Day was celebrated as it is now, although in Scotland this new calendar had been in use since 1600.

NONCONFORMIST RECORDS

Sometimes you cannot find your ancestors in parish registers because they did not belong to the Established Church. Most families have had some connexion with Nonconformity, although it may have been for only a short time. Clues can be found in the presence of marriage entries in a parish register, since after 1754 everyone except Jews and Quakers had to marry in the Established Church. Nonconformists will be found in the marriage registers but not in the registers of baptisms.

From the early seventeenth century many worshippers began to be dissatisfied and broke away from the Established Church to set up sects of their own. At first they were severely treated by the government, but after the Declaration of Indulgence in 1672 Protestant dissenters could apply for licences to have their own meeting houses, and their preachers were granted licences to 'teach'.

The Nonconformist ministers kept informal registers of births, baptisms and burials of members of their chapels, and often took them with them when they moved on to other chapels. In 1840 and 1857 the Registrar General in London ordered that all Nonconformist registers up to 1837 should be deposited with him. The registers are now at the Public Record Office, but some were withheld by the chapels and are still there, or have found their way into County Record Offices. At the Public Record Office there is a list of the deposited registers arranged alphabetically by county, together with the date of foundation of the chapel and its denomination. The list also tells you when the deposited register starts, which may be a good deal later. What set out as a Congregationalist chapel may have ended up

JOHN GREEN =
*of Guddy Bridge, Grasmere,
Co. Westmorland, 1741*

JENNET MACKARETH = **GEORGE GREEN** = **SARAH WILSON**

*servant, 1765,
married 22 September 1765,
buried 23 April 1786
at Grasmere*

*of Goody Bridge, 1766,
Blintern Gill, 1771-1786,
Kitty Crag, 1793-1800,
and Blintern Gill, 1804-
1808, all in Grasmere,
husbandman, baptised
20 September 1741, died
19 March, buried 25 March
1808, at Grasmere, aged 66*

*of Benplace, Grasmere, 1789,
baptised 14 February 1764,
married 18 August 1792, died
19 March, buried 25 March 1808,
at Grasmere, aged 43*

GEORGE GREEN

*baptised 25 July 1768,
buried 6 May 1786, at
Grasmere*

JAMES GREEN

*baptised 14 December
1777, at Grasmere*

MARGARET

*baptised 24 July 1766,
at Grasmere*

BETTY

*baptised 12 February 1771,
at Grasmere*

AGGY

*baptised 9 April 1775,
at Grasmere*

GEORGE GREEN

*baptised 23 December
1798, at Grasmere*

GEORGE GREEN

*baptised 15 November 1829,
at Ambleside, there buried
6 June 1837, aged 7*

THOMAS GREEN = **MARY JANE**

*of Clappersgate,
Co. Westmorland,
1861, gardener, 1858, 1890,
baptised 13 May 1832,
at Ambleside*

*servant, 1858, daughter of
James Routledge, husband-
man, born c.1830, at Penrith,
Co. Cumberland, married
20 November 1858, at Grasmere*

GEORGE GREEN

*baptised 12 June 1859,
at Ambleside*

JAMES GREEN = **SARAH KENNEDY**

*of Church Town, Grasmere, 1890,
slate river, 1890, 1900, slate
quarryman, 1895, born 6 January
1861, at Loughrigg, Grasmere*

*born c.1864, daughter of
Edward Burns, iron miner
married as a widow, 26 March
1890, at the Independent Chapel
of the Wesleyans, Ambleside,
aged 26*

THOMAS EDWARD GREEN

*baptised 17 July 1892,
at Grasmere*

FELIX BURNS GREEN

*born 30 January,
baptised 27 February 1895
at Grasmere*

18   *Six-generation pedigree of the Green family. All the information comes from the parish registers of
Grasmere and Ambleside, and the registers of the Wesleyan Chapel at Ambleside*

JOHN GREEN === JANE JACKSON

JOHN GREEN
of How Head, 1841,
Chapel Hill, 1851,
1861, both in
Ambleside, Co.
Westmorland,
agricultural labourer,
1841, 1861, husbandman,
1858, baptised 12
October 1800 at
Grasmere, aged 50
in 1851, buried
4 March 1891 at
Grasmere, aged 90

JANE JACKSON
born c. 1806 at
Hawkshead,
Co. Lancaster,
married 20 June
1829, at Grasmere,
aged 45 in 1851

WILLIAM GREEN
baptised 19 February,
1804, at Grasmere

THOMAS GREEN
baptised 7 April,
1805 at Grasmere

MARY
in service by 1808
baptised 3 November,
1793, at Grasmere

SARAH
nursemaid at
Dove Cottage,
Grasmere, to
William Wordsworth's
children, 1808,
baptised 8 February
1795, at Grasmere

JANE
baptised 16 October,
1796, at Grasmere

HANNAH
baptised 4 January
1807, at Grasmere

MARY
baptised 7 June 1835,
at Ambleside

SARAH
baptised 11 February 1837,
at Ambleside

DINAH
baptised 19 July 1840,
at Ambleside

JANE
baptised 24 March 1844
at Ambleside

JOHN GREEN
baptised 19 July 1863,
at Grasmere

MARY JANE
baptised 11 May 1865,
at Grasmere

ANN
baptised 16 February 1868,
at Grasmere

JAMES ROUTLEDGE GREEN
baptised 24 September 1896,
at Grasmere

ELIZABETH ANN
baptised 24 July 1898,
at Grasmere

LILY
baptised 29 July 1900,
at Grasmere

in 1837 under another denomination altogether, so you should consult the registers of all the chapels serving your area.

The birth and baptism registers are useful in that they often give the mother's maiden name, and the parents' place of abode and father's occupation in addition to the child's name and date of baptism. It is a good idea to look at the registers covering a wide area around the supposed birthplace of an ancestor, because the family may have travelled some distance to the nearest chapel, or followed a particular preacher. If George and Sarah Green had wanted to attend a Nonconformist chapel they would have had to journey some twelve miles to Kendal.

Between 1742 and 1837 an attempt was made at a voluntary central registration of births. On payment of a small fee parents could register their children's births and be given a certified copy of the entry. Some even registered their own births. The register is held at the Public Record Office, and sometimes it is possible to find Dissenters here who are not mentioned anywhere else, so it is worth having a look at the indices to it.

Each Dissenting chapel also kept a record of admissions of new members and deaths of older ones, besides keeping a written account of what took place at meetings and elections of chapel elders and officials. These are generally still in the chapels, and can add to your knowledge of your family's membership and chapel activities.

QUAKERS

From their beginnings in the middle of the seventeenth century the Society of Friends, or Quakers, kept careful records of all births, marriages and burials reported to their local Monthly Meetings. These records, called Minutes, have been deposited in the Public Record Office, but the Friends' Library in London holds County Digests of Quaker births, marriages and burials down to 1837 containing information taken from the Minutes. Quaker births from 1837 until 1959, deaths up to 1961 and marriages to date are also recorded here in Digests covering the whole country.

The Birth Digests give date of birth, name of the Monthly Meeting to which it was reported, the full names of each child, and his parents, their place of residence, and father's occupation. Marriage Digests contain the date of the Meeting witnessing the marriage, the names and abodes of groom and bride, and their parents' names and abodes. What they do not give, though the original Minutes in the Public Record Office do, are the names and signatures of all those relatives and Friends who were also present. Besides recording the date of interment the Burial Digests list the full names and abode of the dead person, plus his age, and often the names of his parents, and the name of the Monthly Meeting to which his death was reported. These Digests can be much more detailed than parish registers, and if you have Quaker ancestry you should be able to learn much about your family from these and their other records.

The Minutes of the Men's and Women's Meetings, relating to various administrative, judicial and moral matters, can be worth searching. Some have been deposited in County Record Offices, but many are still held by the Monthly Meeting Houses. They met to admit or expel Friends, to enquire into the backgrounds of intending brides and grooms, to receive character references about newcomers, to compose references for Friends leaving the district, and to investigate complaints made among the Friends themselves. As some survive from the mid-seventeenth century they can give you a lot of information about the sort of people your ancestors were and what concerned them.

JEWS

Jewish synagogue registers of births, circumcisions, marriages and burials seldom survive from earlier than the nineteenth century. However, Jews had been settling in England to work or to trade since the mid-seventeenth century. The early immigrants mostly came from Spain and Portugal, but in the nineteenth century they generally came from Central and Eastern Europe, where they had been badly treated. Jewish communities sprang up around the ports of arrival, and where they had no synagogue you can often find births of Jewish people recorded in parish registers. This is because the parish register entry could be used to show a person's age or parentage where inheritance to family property was involved.

Many of the Jewish sources are written in Hebrew, and names given to individuals in synagogue records sometimes differ from the English names used by them. As the Jews settled in England their names were often Anglicized and this adds to the difficulty of identifying immigrants and their families. However, a family's own knowledge of its past or personal documents may help to solve this problem if immigration was within living memory. Sometimes, too, stories of the family's European origins were passed down from generation to generation, enabling you to trace where they came from. Another useful source is the naturalization papers relating to immigrants seeking full British citizenship, and the denization papers, where only partial citizenship was sought. These are held at the Public Record Office and there are typescript indices to them which include any aliases adopted by the applicants. The papers themselves contain much personal detail about these people, particularly where they came from, when and where they were born and married, and the names of their children.

Eastern and Central European Jews normally changed their surnames each generation until forbidden to do so by the laws of their countries. Children took their father or mother's personal name as their surname, so that, for instance, Moses Levi's son David would be called David Moses. Occasionally you will find examples of this in nineteenth century English synagogue records. The Mormons have microfilmed all the German, Polish and Hungarian synagogue records which were discovered to have survived the Second World War. These can be borrowed or viewed at Mormon outlets in England.

The Jewish Museum in London holds original records removed from London synagogues and has a good collection of other material relating to many Jewish families. Besides the synagogue registers there are the membership lists, offering books and legacy lists. The membership lists of Central and East European Jews (called Ashkenasim) were based on synagogue seatholders, while those of the Sephardim (Jews of Spanish and Portuguese origin) were actually regular taxation lists, taken at three-yearly intervals, the assessments being graded according to a person's wealth. These afford a useful directory of Jews living in a specific area. Offering books record donations pledged to the synagogue by male Jews called to read the Scriptures during services, while the legacy lists include the date when bequests were paid to the synagogue and the names of the donors. The legacy list can be used as a starting point for a search for the donor's will, which was generally proved not long before the money was paid out.

Other sources for tracing Jews in this country besides references to them in parish registers, are local newspapers which reported marriages of prosperous Jews, and private collections of papers like the Colyer-Fergusson pedigrees, housed at the Mocatta Library in University College, London.

The Jewish Museum should be able to advise you about other private collections and their whereabouts.

ROMAN CATHOLICS

As Roman Catholics suffered persecution from the mid-sixteenth century at least until the Catholic Relief Act was passed in 1778, it is not surprising that few early registers of baptism and burial survive. This is because the registers would have served as a directory of local Catholics if they had fallen into the wrong hands. Although christened privately by their own priests Catholic children were sometimes taken to the Established Church for a second baptism to avert suspicion and to have some legal record of age and parentage. From the 1790s the Catholics began to keep their own formal registers. Some north country ones have been deposited in the Public Record Office, while others have been copied and printed, or remain in the churches. They are usually written in· Latin, and the baptism registers are interesting because they include the names of godparents as well as those of the child and his real parents, and where they lived.

As you may have difficulty in tracing your family tree from registers if you have Catholic ancestors, the following listings may be of some help: many Roman Catholic families had large estates and from 1715 until 1791 they were forced to register their property with the County Clerk of the Peace. The list of lands registered in 1715 has been published for the whole country and can be used to trace Catholic families and where they lived. The surviving later lists are in the County Record Offices. Lists of Papists, as the Catholics were called, were drawn up for Parliament in 1680, 1705–6, and 1767. These are held by the House of Lords Record Office in London, and they serve as useful directories of people known to be Catholics at these dates, although none is complete for the whole of England and Wales.

Book List

D. Iredale   *Enjoying Archives* 1973

F.G. Emmison   *Archives and Local History* 1974

J.S.W. Gibson   *Record Offices: How to Find Them* 1982

C.R. Humphery-Smith   *Parish Maps of the Counties of England and Wales* 1977

J.S.W. Gibson   *Bishops' Transcripts and Marriage Licences: A Guide to their Location and Indexes* 1982

F.G. Emmison   *How to Read Local Archives 1550–1700* 1978

H.E.P. Grieve   *Examples of English Handwriting 1150–1750* 1966

C.R. Cheney   *Handbook of Dates for Students of English History* 1970

Local Population Studies   *Catalogue of Original Parish Registers in Record Offices and Libraries* 1974, supplements 1976, 1978, 1980, 1982

Society of Genealogists   *Parish Register Copies, Part I: Society of Genealogists Collection* 1983

Society of Genealogists   *Parish Register Copies, Part II: Other than the Society of Genealogists Collection* 1978

Society of Genealogists   *List of Parishes in Boyd's Marriage Index* 1980

CHAPTER FIVE
Church and Churchyard: the Greens

IT IS NOT only books and documents which can help the family historian. The church and churchyard or local cemetery of the place where your ancestors lived can also give you vital information. Even the simplest inscription on a gravestone can fill a missing gap in your family tree. It will tell you the name of the person buried underneath, and his date of death, which you may not have known before. Often his age and the date and place of birth are included, and if the plot of ground belonged to his family, the deaths of his wife and children may also be recorded on the same stone. Several stones clustered together and commemorating one family indicate that a larger plot of ground was reserved for them, and this can help to sort out complicated family relationships where a surname was very common in the parish. The stones may even tell you where the family came from or went to, the names and residences of husbands of female members of the family, and family occupations and educational attainments.

These data can give clues as to which sources to consult next, as well as providing potted biographies not available from any other source. For example, in Grasmere churchyard, close to the path, is a headstone erected 'To the memory of John Hartley who died at Brigham, near Keswick, 26 November 1848, aged 73, also of Agnes his wife, who died at Braithwaite 5 July 1842, aged 67. Also of George and Sarah Green parents of the above Agnes, who perished in the snow on Langdale Fell 19 March 1808, George Green aged 66, Sarah Green aged 43. . . . Also of Jane wife of Wilson Cole and daughter of John and Agnes Hartley, who died 25 August 1879, aged 63 years.' On this one stone is a pedigree of three generations. You can estimate from it approximate birthdates, as well as discover what became of George Green's daughter and where she went to.

ALAN NEVINSON

*19   Interior of Grasmere church. There has probably been a church on this site from the seventh century,
but the oldest part of the present building dates from the thirteenth century. The patron saint is St. Oswald*

The gravestone inscriptions in Grasmere churchyard were copied and printed in the late nineteenth century, so that although some inscriptions are now badly weathered it is possible to know how they read from this transcript.

Until the late eighteenth century, only wealthy landowners and merchants could afford gravestones, which were often very elaborate, and were usually placed inside the church, on the walls, in the floor, or in vaults underneath it. All the inscriptions in Grasmere Church are on the walls, as the floor was bare earth until 1840.

Some of the early memorials took the form of brass panels which are called 'brasses'. They were incised with idealized likenesses of the dead, and bore an inscription about them, normally in Latin.

Tudor and Stuart nobility and gentry were often commemorated by tomb chests. Many were painted and were surrounded by stone canopies. On top of the tombs were sculpted figures of the dead, and the side panels were decorated with small figures representing their children. From these tombs you can learn about contemporary dress, the names and dates of death of the people commemorated, the number and names of their children, and something of the family's supposed origin and history and its role in local and national affairs. If the family was armigerous (i.e., if it had the right to a coat of arms), these arms would also be painted on a shield somewhere on the tomb. They were unique to the family. Sometimes the coat of arms was a complicated one because the family had married into others which were also armigerous, and because the bride was an heiress her arms were incorporated with those of her husband, and passed down to their descendants. There are various books on heraldry which will help you to identify a particular coat of arms and the family to which it belonged, and I have listed a few of them in the book list at the end of this chapter.

From the early eighteenth century wall plaques began to replace the tomb chests. Memorials also began to appear in the churchyard. A wide variety of styles and shapes can be seen even in one churchyard. Local material was generally used, either stone, metal or wood. It depends on the durability of the chosen material, the prevailing local weather conditions, the depth to which the letters in the inscriptions were carved, and the way in which the churchyards were kept as to how legible even fairly recent gravestones are. You may find that some stones have sunk into the ground, or have been overtaken by frost, weeds or lichen, while others are almost as readable as the day they were put up three or more centuries ago.

In Scotland many churchyards contain pre-seventeenth century gravestones dedicated to local inhabitants of all ranks. They often record residence, occupation and place of origin, and occasionally names of nearer ancestors. This is very helpful, because Scottish burial registers are not complete. Although many Scottish churchyards have been abandoned or are situated in remote places, a reasonable number of inscriptions have been copied and printed. The Scottish Record Office and New

Register House in Edinburgh have collections of these transcripts, as has the Society of Genealogists in London.

Only a small proportion of English and Welsh gravestone inscriptions have been printed. They can be seen in County Record Offices and the library of the Society of Genealogists. A partial survey of Irish headstones is contained in the volumes of the *Journal of the Association for the Preservation of Memorials of the Dead in Ireland*, issued from 1892 onwards.

Public cemeteries are also worth a visit. They took over when the churchyards became overcrowded. They are owned and run by City, Borough or District Councils, and private Companies, which hold their own registers of burials, cemetery plans and lists of plot numbers. The official in charge should be able to locate the grave of a particular person from these records. At Grasmere bodies were taken to the village cemetery to be buried from 1892, except where partly walled or earthen graves in the churchyard could be opened to a depth of five feet without disturbing human remains or exposing coffins, so that relatives could be interred there.

INSIDE THE CHURCH

Besides wall plaques and memorials there are other things to interest the family historian inside the church. If there is a printed guide available this should tell you something about the history of the parish, its chief inhabitants, and benefactors. Some churches have a special Benefactors' Board hanging on the wall listing names of parishioners who gave money or land to help support the poor or orphaned. You may also see a Book of Remembrance or War Memorial tablet containing the names and ranks of men and women who died in the two World Wars. If you can look at an old Parish Magazine or local newspaper of the time you should be able to discover more about these people from their obituaries and death notices. There should be a store of older Magazines either in the church or at the vicarage or rectory. At Grasmere I found old monthly Parish Magazines ranging between January 1896 and 1920. These contained baptisms, marriages and burials of parishioners, awards of School attendance medals and prizes, reports on parish events and activities, decisions taken at Vestry Meetings, the distribution of money from local charities, and fund-raising efforts.

Inside the church there would once have been a parish chest. This had to be paid for out of parish funds, taken from church collections. The chest had at least two locks, and the parish registers and other important parish documents were stored there for safekeeping. Most of the documents date from the late sixteenth century or later. They include books recording the minutes of Vestry Meetings, Churchwardens' Accounts, Highway Surveyors' Accounts, deeds or wills relating to gifts of money or land to the church, the Poor Rate Books and Accounts of the Overseers of the Poor, and other loose papers concerning paupers. Many of these are still kept in the church, but some have been transferred to County Record Offices, and others have been lost or destroyed.

From the Middle Ages the church was the centre of the community. It regulated people's lives, and obliged them to attend the numerous church services and to perform certain parish duties, on pain of fine or public penance. The church was run by various officials who were elected from among the parishioners. Elections took place annually. It was at the Easter meeting of the Vestry that the churchwardens were elected for the year. The Vestry consisted of a selected group of inhabitants, or was made up of all the ratepayers in the parish. Grasmere had a 'select' Vestry of eighteen representatives from its four townships. Once selected they could remain members for life. The Vestry was replaced in 1894 by the Parish Church Council. The Minutes of the Vestry meetings record how the parish was run, the orders made for maintenance against reputed fathers of bastard children, the fines and penances meted out for misbehaviour, decisions affecting the financial management of the church and the collection of rates.

The Churchwardens' Accounts reveal a wide range of duties. They contain entries of payments made to local workmen for repairs to and upkeep of the church buildings, and to craftsmen for making and repairing church furniture, and they record sums collected for special reasons such as to help the inhabitants of another parish hit by flood or fire. Recorded too are the amounts paid to parishioners for killing sparrows and other vermin which attacked crops and animals, so even if your ancestors were never elected churchwardens they may well have been mentioned in records like these.

There were six churchwardens for Grasmere parish. Two were elected for Grasmere township, two for Langdale township, and one each for the township of Rydal and Loughrigg, and for part of Ambleside. Each township undertook to maintain a particular part of the church, and to share general costs for the upkeep of the church tower, the bells, the roof, and the furniture. The Accounts appear to survive only from 1790, although a few sporadic entries were written into the parish registers from the seventeenth century onwards.

The Accounts show that George Green was chosen as churchwarden for Grasmere township at Easter 1795, 1797 and 1805. Part of his expenditure in 1797 was ninepence paid to mend the schoolhouse lock and key (the school was endowed by various benefactors whose money was used to pay the schoolmaster's salary, while the schoolhouse was maintained by the parish). A typical year's Accounts included the cost of ringing and greasing the church bells, dressing the church and church-yard, cleaning the church windows and Sentences (these were wooden boards inscribed with religious texts and hung inside the church), washing the church linen, mending the steeple window, paying the dog-whipper to whip out any dogs

ALAN NEVINSON

20   Extract from the churchwardens' accounts for the parish of Grasmere. George Green was elected as churchwarden at a vestry meeting on Easter Tuesday 1805. He served for a year. None of the six churchwardens was paid for his year in office

which strayed into church during the services, the rushbearers to remove and replace rushes laid on the earthen floor of the church (payment took the form of ale, but from 1829 gingerbread seems to have been given instead), drawing up a copy of the parish register (the Bishop's Transcript), and the churchwardens' own expenses for taking and vacating office and for making presentments to the Archdeacon on certain matters relating to the parish.

The two Highway Surveyors were elected annually by the local magistrates, on the recommendation of the Vestry. Every year the Surveyors took their Accounts to the County Quarter Sessions for inspection by the magistrates. The Surveyors' duty was to keep the roads running through the parish in good repair. Until 1835 every male inhabitant was supposed to do one day's work a year on the roads, but he could opt out by paying a fine which was then used to pay the cost of hiring professional labour. From 1835 a special highway rate was levied for this purpose, and the upkeep of the roads became the responsibility of highway district authorities, made up of clusters of parishes. The Highway Surveyors' Accounts contain the amounts spent on the roads and the names of those people paid to repair them. The Grasmere Accounts show that in 1844 John Green was paid two shillings and threepence for leading two carts of 'covers' from White Moss Quarry. This would have been slate, slabs of which would have been used to cover ditches crossed by the road, and pavements.

Two Overseers of the Poor were elected every year by the local magistrates from names supplied to them by the Vestry. Often they were also the churchwardens. Their Poor Rate Books date from 1691 and run up to 1834, when supervision of poor relief passed to the Poor Law Commission in London. The Books record the regular receipts of money from householders in the parish, the sum paid being based on the value of the land a person occupied. They show a person's comparative wealth in relation to his neighbours', as well as the period during which he paid the rates. The Overseers' Account Books show the dates and reasons why a person received temporary or permanent help either in the form of cash, work, clothes, or apprenticeship at the parish expense. The Accounts were reviewed at regular intervals, and new names added, and others removed. Unfortunately I could not find any old Rate Books or Overseers' Accounts in Grasmere Church.

Each parish had a constable who had a variety of duties. These included maintaining the parish stocks and cage (where people were confined for short periods as a punishment for offences like giving false weights and measures), helping the churchwardens to present for punishment people who failed to attend church services, inspecting alehouses and suppressing gaming-houses, collecting the county rate and acting as agent for the collection of other national taxes, calling parish meetings, caring for the parish bull, supervising the welfare of the poor, and helping with the removal of strangers refused a legal settlement in the parish. As the constable's job brought him into contact with nearly everyone in the parish, the post was not very popular. He was elected by the local magistrates and served for a year. At Grasmere a written agreement was made on 13th January 1712 (1713 modern style) by the inhabitants and landholders that the office should be taken in turn and that they hoped the magistrates would agree to this. A list of the landholders and their property followed, which is useful because it tells us who lived where in the parish at that time.

Among loose papers relating to the poor which you may be lucky enough to find in the parish chest are the agreements made between the Overseers of the Poor and local people concerning boys and girls put out to them as apprentices. They were taken on at the age of seven or eight and retained until they reached twenty-four or were married, whichever happened first. These children came from families who were too poor to support them, and they normally went into farm or domestic service.

Between 1691 and 1834 any newcomers to the parish who looked as if they might need financial help were examined on oath as to their circumstances by the Overseers of the Poor in the presence of a local magistrate. Especially vulnerable were large families, elderly folk and people without any obvious source of income. They were questioned about their birthplace, parish of apprenticeship, and last place of employment for a year or more, because whichever was the latest of these conferred a legal place of settlement. If it was felt desirable the stranger could be immediately returned there, escorted by the parish constable. Legal settlement was also granted by the parish where an individual intermarried with a native, or where the head of the family held property worth at least £10 a year, or contributed to the parish rates. After the examination the answers were signed or marked by the newcomer and his examiners, and filed in the parish chest. Either he would then be allowed to settle in the parish or a Removal Order would be drafted, giving the name of the parish where he was last legally settled and to which he was to be returned. This Order was given by the constable to his counterpart on arrival.

These papers are good sources of background information about newcomers to a parish because they trace their life stories and movements about the country and abroad. Often, though, the papers were destroyed to make way for other parish material in the parish chest, and I did not find any relating to Grasmere.

Each parish belonged to a deanery, which itself was part of an archdeaconry. From Medieval times the Archdeacon regularly visited the parishes in his care and set a series of questions for the incumbent and the parish officials to answer about the state of the church building, and the moral state of the parishioners. The records of these Archdeacons' Visitations are filed among other ecclesiastical papers in the Diocesan Registry, and can add interest to your family history where it lived in a parish for a considerable length of time.

Booklist
J. West   *Village Records* 1962, reprinted 1982
J. Richardson   *The Local Historian's Encyclopaedia* 1981
L.M. Munby   *Short Guides to Records* 1962
W.E. Tate   *The Parish Chest* 1978

H.L. White   *Monuments and their Inscriptions* 1978
J.P. Brooke-Little   *An Heraldic Alphabet* 1973
A.C. Fox-Davies   *Armorial Families* 1970
J.B. Burke   *The General Armory of England, Scotland, Ireland and Wales* 1884

CHAPTER SIX

Local Records and Wills: the Greens

GEORGE AND SARAH Green's second son John lived until he was ninety years old. He was buried at Grasmere on 14th March 1891. To find out more about him, I looked at the local newspaper, *The Westmorland Gazette*, for the week ending on 14th March. It reported that 'On Monday last at Grasmere a well known character passed away in the person of Old John Green. . . . The tragic end of his parents made John a well known character and he was almost the oldest person in the place . . . having been baptized at Grasmere on 12 October 1800. He has lived within the ancient parish ever since only sleeping out of it on two occasions. For many years he lived at Ambleside, and while working there for Mr Benson Harrison he was so seriously injured as to be disabled from work ever after. He was leading two carts of coals, when the horses were startled by a rifle shot over the road, and bolted, knocking John down and severely mangling his body. His strong constitution enabled him to recover and for the past 30 years he lived on a pension of 5/- a week paid by Benson Harrison and his representatives. . . . He lived with his son Mr Thomas Green. There now remains but one of the six orphan children alive, Mrs Hannah Hall, who lives with her son and grandchildren at Score Crag which overlooks the old homestead which has long since passed into other hands.'

Provincial newspapers are an excellent source for the family historian, especially from the late nineteenth century when they started to report mostly local news. However, you do need to have a good idea when a person was born, married or died, or when a particular family event took place, as local newspapers usually appear at least once a week. You can find out which newspapers served your area from one of the printed guides included in the book list at the end of the chapter. Your library should have a stock of back numbers of local newspapers. Besides births, marriages

BY PERMISSION OF THE TRUSTEES OF DOVE COTTAGE

21   *John Green and his sister Hannah Hall. This photograph was taken in 1890 in front of the cottage at Blintern Gill. John was then aged 89 and Hannah 83, WLMS 5/10/163*

and deaths, obituaries, local news and events, property sales, Coroners' Inquests into sudden deaths, and tradesmen's advertisements were included.

From the parish registers and the Census Returns I knew already that John Green had been a labourer, that his son Thomas was baptized on 13th May 1832 at Ambleside, and that he became a gardener living at Clappersgate around the time of his father's accident in 1861. Hannah Green married Anthony Hall at Grasmere on 17th February 1845 and had four children by him, the last born when she was forty-six years old. Anthony was buried on 29th October 1886, aged 89, but Hannah survived until January 1897, when she was buried at Grasmere aged 91. The son she went to live with was called William Hall, a hind by occupation, and his wife was also named Hannah.

TRADE DIRECTORIES

Local trade and commercial directories are also worth consulting. From the late eighteenth century private firms began to publish County and City Directories of names and addresses of private residents, and those of professional and tradespeople. You can find out the years in which a directory was published for your county and the name of its publisher from one of the two printed guides in the book list. Many County Record Offices and local reference libraries have good runs of local directories, while the Guildhall Library in London has a large collection of directories extending over the whole country.

Provincial directories were divided up into sections, according to Parliamentary Wards and then alphabetically by the villages and townships within each Ward. Not every householder's name appeared, so the directories are not fully comprehensive, but they can be useful in locating the exact address of recorded people round about a Census year, especially if they lived in a large town or city. By looking at a sequence of directories you can discover how long a person lived at a particular place and whether his business was continued by later generations of his family.

I looked at Parson and White's *History, Directory and Gazetteer of Cumberland and Westmorland*, issued in 1829, for entries in the name of Green at Grasmere and Ambleside. No trace was found of John Green, although his employer, Benson Harrison, was recorded as residing at Green Bank, Ambleside. From the *Directory* I learned that Ambleside had a large woollen mill at this time, as well as a tannery and a corn mill.

POLL BOOKS AND ELECTORAL REGISTERS

Before 1832 only a small minority of people in Britain were entitled to vote for Members of Parliament. The right depended on ownership of land worth over a certain amount. By the nineteenth century the system was breaking down. The Reform Act of 1832 tidied matters up but most of the population were still left without a vote. Throughout the later nineteenth century the franchise was gradually extended, although women were excluded until 1918.

From 1695 up to the mid-nineteenth century County Poll Books were published after every Parliamentary election. The Books listed the names of all those people qualified to vote, arranged under the towns and villages where their qualifying land lay. If they resided somewhere else their place of abode was included. There was no secret ballot until 1872, so although the Poll Books recorded the way a person voted, this did not always reflect his real political views, because voters were often subject to pressure from wealthy local landowners with a vested interest in who was elected to Parliament to represent them. The Poll Books are a directory of the more affluent members of the community, showing which people held land worth over a certain value, and they predate Directories by over a century. Many Poll Books have found their way into County Record Offices, and the Guildhall Library in London has an extensive collection of them for the whole country.

In 1832 the franchise was extended to more people, and annual Electoral Registers were compiled and printed, listing persons entitled to vote within each Parliamentary Division. Local ones can be seen at County Record Offices and afford a useful guide to landholders in the area. Each voter was given an electoral number, and the Registers record his address, the name and nature of the qualifying property and whether it was occupied by a tenant. In the 1841 Electoral Register of Westmorland I found that Benson Harrison, of Green Bank, Ambleside, was entitled to vote because he held a freehold house and land in Ambleside. His electoral number was 2314. Apparently none of the Greens was qualified to vote as their names were not recorded in the Register.

MAPS

Maps can help to pinpoint a family's homestead, as well as those of neighbours, their relative size and shape of holding, and the roads, tracks and streams which served them. Ordnance Survey maps on a scale of one inch to the mile began to be regularly published from 1805, and a series of larger scale maps, of six inches to the mile and of twenty-five inches to the mile, was first issued between 1856 and 1860. If you are lucky enough to see one of these larger scale maps in your County Record Office or Library then it will be much more detailed and will include field names not mentioned on a one-inch map.

If you have found your ancestors in the 1841 Census Returns, scrutiny of the parish Tithe Map and Apportionment will show exactly where they lived about that time. Between 1836 and 1842 each parish in England and Wales was surveyed by specially appointed Tithe Redemption Commissioners so that an annual tax called the Tithe could be changed from payment in kind to a sum of money. The amount depended on the annual value of the land a person occupied and the current price of corn. A map was drawn up showing the boundaries of each landholding in the parish, and every holding was given a number. The Apportionment matched up these numbers with the names of the owners and occupiers of the plots, together with a description of the land and premises, their state of cultivation and their size. Three copies of the Map and Apportionment were made. Because the Tithe had been paid to the Incumbent of the parish to boost his income, one copy was kept in the church, another was deposited with the Diocesan Registrar and the third was filed in the Tithe Redemption Commission. The Public Record Office at Kew now has all the Maps and Apportionments once in the custody of the Tithe Redemption Commission, while many of the other copies have been placed in County Record Offices.

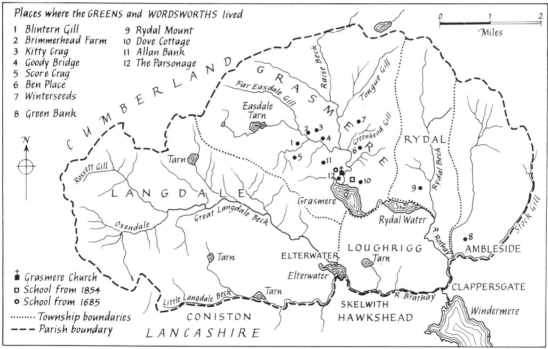

22   A map of the parish of Grasmere, showing where the Green and Wordsworth families lived

Another important group of maps are the ones attached to Enclosure Awards. Originally each parish had a stretch of common and waste land where anyone in the parish could take what grew there or use the land for grazing. From the sixteenth century local landlords began to fence in the common land for their own agricultural purposes. This caused hardship among the other inhabitants although they were supposed to be consulted before enclosure took place. During the eighteenth century many landlords overrode their tenants' wishes by petitioning Parliament to grant them private Acts to allow them to enclose the common land. From 1801 onwards enclosure was very strictly regulated and could be carried out only by Act of Parliament. While the Bill was going through Parliament parishioners could put forward their objections to enclosure. Petitions, Bills, objections to them, and the enrolled Acts are held by the House of Lords Library in London. Most of the maps marking out enclosure before 1801 and between 1836 and 1844 are held in County Record Offices, while maps drafted between 1801 and 1835 and after 1845 have been deposited in the Public Record Office at Kew.

The maps mark out the plots of land already held and those to be allotted as a result of enclosure. The Awards set out the names of owners and occupiers of each plot, their size, state of cultivation and annual value, and the plots to be awarded in compensation for the loss of use of commons, based on the size and value of the present holding. Like the Tithe Maps these can indicate exactly where people lived and what their property was used for.

MANORIAL RECORDS

From the early Middle Ages up until the early twentieth century the land was divided into manors, each with its own landlord. Manorial and parish boundaries do not always coincide, so that one parish might have been divided up among several manors. You can find out which manors your parish belonged to from the County Record Office or from a printed local history. The Historical Manuscripts Commission in London has a slip index of English and Welsh manors, giving the whereabouts and types of all known records relating to them. The written records kept by the landlords included rentals, Court Minute Books and Rolls, maps, and manorial surveys. Some of these go as far back as the thirteenth century. Up until 1732 they were written in Latin, except for a short period during the Commonwealth, 1653–1660, when they were in English.

The landlord, or his deputy, the Steward, collected rents from the tenants, who also had to perform certain services like maintaining roads and hedges running through the manor, keeping ditches clear, and repairing fences. The lord usually held a meeting of his Court at least twice a year. Every tenant had to attend unless he had a reasonable excuse. The Court was known as the Court Leet. It met to fine or punish tenants who had committed petty offences such as slander, brawling or eavesdropping, and to appoint manorial officials for the year, like the aletaster and the manorial constable. The work of the manorial officials thus often overlapped with that of the parish officials.

Often the Court Leet was combined with the General Court Baron, and the

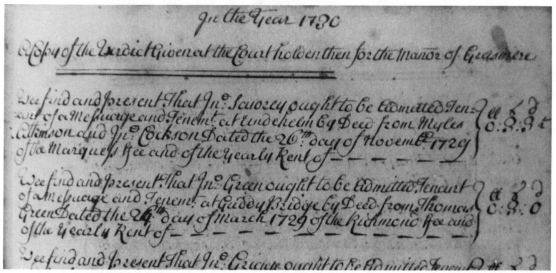

ALAN NEVINSON

23 *Part of the proceedings at the Manorial Court of Grasmere, which were found among parish records in the church. It reads:*

In the Year 1730
A Copy of the Verdict Given at the Court holden then for the Manor of Grasmere.

Wee find and present that Jn° Green ought to be Admitted Tenant of a Messuage and Tenemt. at Guddy Bridge by Deed from Thomas Green Dated the 24(?)th day of March 1729 of the Richmond ffee and of the Yearly Rent of £0:8s:0d

Minutes of both meetings were recorded together in a Book or on a Roll. The Court Baron recorded transfers of land from one tenant to another. Before this could be done the land had to be formally surrendered back to the lord of the manor. He then admitted the new tenant and charged him an entry 'fine'. The tenant was given a copy of the entry in the Court Minutes as proof of his right to occupy the land. For this reason he was called a copyholder.

The Minutes also contain summaries of land transfers called leases. These date from the late seventeenth century. A lease was a gift or sale of land for a fixed period or for a number of specified lives. The deed was called an Indenture because of the wavy line which was cut between the two identical copies given to the purchaser and retained by the seller. The Indentures give a lot of information about the date and terms of the agreement, the site, nature and annual value of the property, and the price paid for it, as well as being signed by the parties at the bottom. They also give details of any tenants already occupying the property, and sometimes the names of people on whose land the property abutted. Some of these Indentures have found their way into County Record Offices, but as they were private agreements many have disappeared or have been destroyed, and the Court Baron Minutes may be the only record we have that such a transaction took place.

WILLS

Wills are another very useful source of biographical information. A will contains the written instructions of the testator about what is to happen to his land after his death. A testament expresses his wishes about his goods and chattels. The two are usually combined in one document called a will and testament. The testator signs the will at the bottom, in front of two witnesses who also sign in his presence at the same time.

After his death the executors appointed by him in his will produce the document at a District Probate Registry to be proved. The will is then filed in the Registry and a copy given to the executors to allow them to carry out the instructions contained in it. Since 1858 English and Welsh wills have been proved in the Principal Probate Registry in London and in over forty District Registries. The Registry most convenient to the executors is normally used, regardless of where the testator lived. The original wills are sent to the Principal Probate Registry, where they can be consulted on payment of a fee. There are yearly indices to them, which tell you when and where the will was proved, the date and place of the testator's death, the names and addresses of his executors and the total value of his estate.

Before 1858 wills were taken to the ecclesiastical courts to be proved; the earliest series of wills dates from 1383. There were several kinds of ecclesiastical court. Generally if a person held lands and goods in one Archdeaconry then the executors took his will to the Archdeaconry Court for probate. If his lands and goods were spread over several Archdeaconries within one diocese then the will would be proved in the Bishop's Consistory Court. If the lands and goods were scattered over several dioceses then the appropriate Archbishop's Court was used. This was the general rule, but you should always scan the indices of wills proved in all the courts serving the area. There were also a host of little probate courts outside this system, called Peculiars, so you will need to know whether there were any in your area.

In Ireland wills were proved in ecclesiastical courts until 1857, the highest being the Prerogative Court of the Archbishop of Armagh. From 1858 these courts were replaced by the civil Probate Registries under the Principal Probate Registry in Dublin. Nearly all the Prerogative Court of Armagh wills were consumed by fire in 1922, but there are abstracts of wills proved between 1536 and 1800 which were made by Sir William Betham, and the Society of Genealogists in London has microfilms of these.

Before 1560 Scottish testaments were confirmed by commissaries in ecclesiastical courts called commissariots. The boundaries of the commissariots were the same as the bishoprics. After 1560 the Crown administered the commissariots and the Principal Commissary Court was in Edinburgh. From 1809 the provincial commissariots gradually began to be administered by sheriffs and their clerks, and in 1823 the boundaries were merged with the sheriffdoms. Finally in 1876 the Commissariots were abolished and replaced by the Sheriff Courts.

to the Trusteeship **And I declare** *that the powers and* &c &c
discretions hereinbefore vested in the Trustees hereinbefore named as
shall be exerciseable by the Trustees or Trustee for the time being of
my Will **Lastly** *I hereby revoke all other Wills* **In Witness** *and*
whereof I have hereunder subscribed my name this Thirtyfirst August
~~*day of*~~ ———————— *in the year of our Lord one thousand eight* &c &c
hundred and forty seven

Signed *by the Testator William Wordsworth*
is his last Will and Testament in the presence
of us present at the same time who at
his request in his presence and in the
presence of each other hereunto subscribe
our names as Witnesses ————————

William Wordsworth

24 *The end of the will of William Wordsworth, made on 31 August 1847, signed by him and Benson Harrison as one of the two witnesses. The will was proved at London, with one codicil, on 27 May 1850, Wordsworth having died the month before* PROB 1/90

You can find out the names of the courts and the whereabouts of Irish and Scottish wills and testaments from the printed guide in the book list.

What do wills contain? A will is headed by the name, address and occupation of the testator, usually followed by the date when it was made, although this sometimes appears at the end, just before the testator's signature. He mentions those lands and goods that he wishes to leave to particular people and sometimes records how he came by them himself, perhaps by marriage or as a beneficiary of someone else's will. Some wills are very lengthy and have later additions, called codicils. You should always read the entire will, because it can be a goldmine of information.

When you make a summary of the will, always word your notes as if you were the testator: for instance, write 'my son' as the testator did. This is because in some wills family relationships can be extraordinarily involved. You can avoid further misunderstanding by copying down the details exactly as they appeared.

If someone died without making a will the Court could appoint a person to administer the estate of the deceased. This person was normally the next of kin. He was granted letters of administration. The grants are often indexed with the wills and they give the dead person's name, address and occupation, the date of the grant, the name of the person to whom the grant was made and his relationship to the deceased. From 1858 the date and place of death of the deceased were included too.

75

INVENTORIES

Another series of documents which tell you something about what your ancestors possessed are the Inventories drawn up after their deaths. Until 1782 they were obligatory. An Inventory listed a person's goods in and about his house with their saleable value. It was generally made within a few days of his death so that if his property had to be sold to pay off his debts, or the legacies made in his will, it could be established that he would have enough cash. The Inventory was deposited in the appropriate ecclesiastical court. Because of their nature Inventories can give us a good picture of a person's home and how it was furnished, as well as itemising his working tools.

TAXATION LISTS

A person's status and place of abode at a particular date can sometimes be gleaned from taxation lists. Some of the early taxes seem strange to us. For instance, from 1662 until 1689 a tax was imposed at regular intervals on hearths. Every householder had to pay two shillings for each of his hearths. Local officials drew up a list of taxpayers in every hamlet, village and town in England and Wales, together with the number of hearths each person had to pay for. Copies of the lists were sent to London and are now in the Public Record Office in London. They are grouped by county and by the year in which the tax was levied. I found that in the Hearth Tax Return for Westmorland in 1670 there were four Green households among the forty-eight assessed to pay in Grasmere.

No. of Register.	Names of Proprietors.	Names of Occupiers.	Sums Assessed.			Date of Contract.
			£.	s.	d.	
38035	Cath: Wilson —	Self — — —		1	2	
	Agnes Walker —	Do. — — —		4	10	18 May 1799
	Geo: Green — — —	Do. — — —			9	Oct.o 1799

25 *Part of the land tax assessment for the township of Grasmere, 1799. George Green was an owner-occupier and was assessed to pay ninepence on his property, Blintern Gill. IR 23/93 Crown copyright*

In 1697 the Land Tax was first raised. It was based on the value of the land a person occupied. The lists of names were arranged in the same way as the Hearth Tax Returns, but gave the amounts due from each person. Most of the surviving lists are held in County Record Offices; few date from earlier than the end of the eighteenth century. From 1782 the landowner's name was included, so you can discover whether your ancestor occupied his own land or was a tenant of someone else.

Other taxation lists which you may find in County Record Offices concern levies on windows between 1696 and 1851, carriages between 1747 and 1782, silver plate between 1756 and 1777, male servants between 1775 and 1852, horses between 1784 and 1874, game between 1784 and 1807, heraldic coats of arms between 1793 and 1882, dogs between 1796 and 1882 and uninhabited houses between 1851 and 1924. You would be very lucky to locate all of these, or to find runs of names extending over the entire period when the various taxes were collected. Another important thing to remember is that not everyone was taxed, so if a person's name does not appear in a taxation list for a particular place it does not necessarily mean that he did not live there at that time.

Between 1710 and 1811 a tax was imposed on the premium paid to masters taking on apprentices to learn a trade or craft. The tax due depended on the amount of the premium and had to be paid to the Inland Revenue within a year after the apprenticeship was completed. Apprenticeship Books containing details of apprentices bound during this period are held at the Public Record Office at Kew. They are arranged by date and list many thousands of names. The Society of Genealogists in London has a typescript copy of the entries to 1774 arranged alphabetically by the name of the apprentice, and to 1762 by the name of the master. Up to 1751 the Books recorded not only the apprentice's name but also that of his father or guardian, his residence and occupation. Then followed the master's name, address and trade, the length of the apprenticeship and the premium paid for the training. You can thus learn a boy's place of origin from these Books, as well as his paternity, and the trade he was set to. Often a boy was placed with a relative or family friend far from home, so you should not ignore the name and address of the master when carrying out research for a person apprenticed during these years, because information about them can sometimes add to your family's history.

FAMILY PAPERS

Private papers and documents of more substantial and landed local families often find their way into County Record Offices. They record family affairs, business and estate administration. Letters, journals, diaries, bills and receipts help to build up a picture of the everyday life not only of the family concerned but of the community in which they thrived. Although your family may not have amassed a collection of such material, their names may be mentioned in someone else's writings. A good example of this is the information about the fate of the Green children, which I discovered from Dorothy Wordsworth's papers.

In April 1808, William Wordsworth persuaded Dorothy to write *A Narrative concerning George and Sarah Green of the Parish of Grasmere*. Although not published until 1936, it was preserved by the Wordsworth family. According to the Narrative, when neighbours entered Blintern Gill shortly after the bodies were found they discovered only two boilings of potatoes, a very small amount of meal, a little bread, and three or four legs of dried lean mutton by way of food for the six children and their missing parents. No money was found in the house. To provide them with milk the family kept an old cow, which fetched twenty-four shillings at an auction of the house contents held later. The place was then left empty.

Apparently it was the custom of the parish to make a weekly allowance of two shillings towards the support of destitute orphans under ten. The five youngest Green children were under this age, and within a month the children had been found homes in the village. Of the eight offspring the two oldest girls were already in service; George, born in 1798, was taken into his older half-brother's house at Ambleside to be brought up in his business as a weaver; John, born in 1800, was to be cared for by his sister Jane's godfather, John Fleming, a farmer in Grasmere. The two youngest sons, William and Thomas, were taken into the house of Mrs Dawson, at Benplace in Grasmere, while Jane and the baby, Hannah, went to the house of John Watson, the blacksmith at Winterseeds. His mother had been sister to George Green's first wife, Jennet Mackareth.

In addition to the parish allowance, a public subscription fund was opened. The parish clerk, George Mackereth, was appointed the official collector and the Rector was nominated Trustee. He held the moneys. Six ladies of the parish, including William Wordsworth's wife Mary, were asked to supervise the collection, administer the funds and arrange for the provision of food and clothing for the children, their education, and their final setting up in work. A special Subscription Book was kept in which were written the names of donors and the amounts they had paid into the fund. From Dorothy Wordsworth's correspondence I found that subscriptions to the fund had exceeded £300 by May 1800, less than two months after the tragedy. To help give publicity to the fund her brother William wrote a short narrative describing the event and circulated it among his friends in London and elsewhere.

Originally it was hoped to erect a tombstone over the grave of George and Sarah Green, but the Fund Committee decided that more necessary things should be settled first "before anything were introduced into the concern which to common-place minds might appear like a fancy or a luxury". As we saw in Chapter 5, it was the family of George's daughter Agnes who finally placed a gravestone in the churchyard.

Once the Committee felt that enough money had been raised to provide for the orphans' upkeep and futures the fund was closed, to prevent their becoming more wealthy than was good for them, and to avoid any feelings of envy among their neighbours.

On 25th May 1829 seven children, plus their half-brother James Green who had looked after George, came to Rydal Mount to receive their equal shares from the £536 taken from the sale of investments out of the fund. By then George was working at Hendon in Middlesex, and did not attend. The receipts, signed or marked by the children, were filed among the rest of the papers relating to the fund.

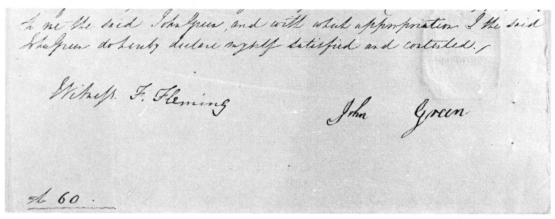

BY PERMISSION OF THE TRUSTEES OF DOVE COTTAGE

26 John Green's receipt for £60, paid on 25 May 1829 in final settlement of the Green Fund 'raised for the relief, maintenance, bringing up, and putting out into the world of the children of George and Sarah Green'
WLMS 5/10/188

As you can see, often the most rewarding documents are in your own house if you know where to look and what to look for. In the case of Dorothy Wordsworth I was lucky because she was very interested in village affairs and kept a detailed daily record of them, and was in the habit of writing letters to her many friends and relatives. A good number of these have survived and have been printed or made available to the public.

Book List
Willings Press Guide
The Times Tercentenary Handlist of English and Welsh Newspapers, Magazines and Reviews 1620–1920 1920
J.E. Norton *Guide to National and Provincial Directories of England and Wales, excluding London, published before 1856 1950*
C.W.F. Goss *The London Directories 1677–1855 1932*
A.J. Camp *Wills and their Whereabouts 1974*

CHAPTER SEVEN
School and Work: the Greens

THE HEADMASTER, WILLIAM Fuller, wrote the following entry in the Log Book of Grasmere Elementary School on 22nd May 1874: "Last evening I kept John Green in until half past four to write a punishment. Finding today that he neither stayed in nor did the punishment and this being the second offence I caned him." According to the School Register of Admissions, which survives from 1864, the hapless John Green was admitted as a pupil on 18th May 1874. He was the son of Thomas Green of Broadgate, Grasmere, and was born on 23rd May 1863. His two older brothers and sister Ann also went to the school, and he left on 22nd June 1877 when he was fourteen years old. Poring over the pages of the Log Book, I found out about the size of the classes, what lessons they were taught, prevailing weather conditions, and absences due to illness or other causes. In the summer the children were often kept away by their parents to help with harvesting and sheep clipping.

Every schoolmaster kept a Register of Admissions of new pupils, and a Log Book recording the daily events in the school. Although few Log Books have been copied and printed, a number of the more famous public and grammar school Admission Registers have been published. Some even say what became of the boys after they left the school. If the Register has not been published the County Archivist may be able to tell you its whereabouts. Of course if the school still exists it is probable that the early Register has remained in its custody, but if the school has long since disappeared, then the chances are that the records have disappeared with it.

When they left school most children found work locally. In Grasmere farming was the most important occupation. George Green, who perished in the snow in 1808, was a husbandman, and his son John was described as an agricultural servant in 1851, and a husbandman in 1858. George lived on his own smallholding at Blintern

80

FROM THE COLLECTION OF MRS CATHERINE THOMPSON

27 A photograph of the pupils of Grasmere Elementary School about 1900. Thomas Edward Green, son of John Green, is second from the left in the front row. The headmaster, William Fuller, ran the school from 1864 to 1908

Gill, but it was not big enough to give him a decent income. The local custom of splitting up a dead person's lands among his family eventually reduced them to being incapable of supporting a family at all. George Green boosted his earnings by digging up peat from his land to sell to his neighbours for fuel. The sort of farming he would have done was mixed, growing vegetables like potatoes and turnips, and possibly oats and barley, and grazing a few sheep (probably Herdwicks and Swaledales) and dairy cattle such as Galloways and Longhorns. Before his death the family had already sold their horse and kept only an old cow to provide them with milk.

George Green's son John was an agricultural servant in 1851, according to the Census. He would have done general work around the farm and was probably not attached to any particular farmer, getting work where he could. By 1851 an agricultural labourer earned about eleven shillings a week, and the rent of a cottage was between fifty and sixty shillings a year. In Westmorland most unmarried labourers boarded and lodged at the farmhouse, and were hired for six months at a

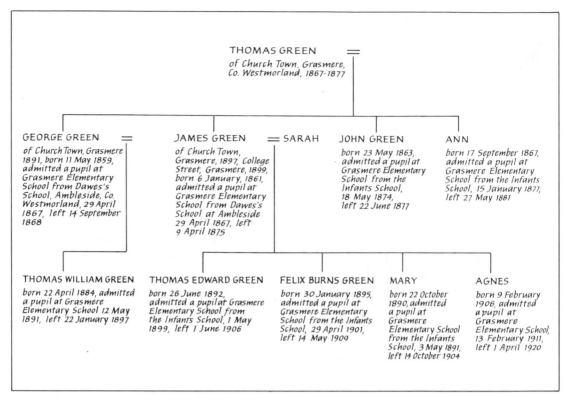

THOMAS GREEN =
of Church Town, Grasmere,
Co. Westmorland, 1867-1877

GEORGE GREEN =
of Church Town, Grasmere,
1891, born 11 May 1859,
admitted a pupil at
Grasmere Elementary
School from Dawes's
School, Ambleside, Co.
Westmorland, 29 April
1867, left 14 September
1868

JAMES GREEN = SARAH
of Church Town,
Grasmere, 1897, College
Street, Grasmere, 1899,
born 6 January, 1861,
admitted a pupil at
Grasmere Elementary
School from Dawes's
School at Ambleside
29 April 1867, left
9 April 1875

JOHN GREEN
born 23 May 1863,
admitted a pupil at
Grasmere Elementary
School from the
Infants School,
18 May 1874,
left 22 June 1877

ANN
born 17 September 1867,
admitted a pupil at
Grasmere Elementary
School from the Infants
School, 15 January 1877,
left 27 May 1881

THOMAS WILLIAM GREEN
born 22 April 1884, admitted
a pupil at Grasmere
Elementary School 12 May
1891, left 22 January 1897

THOMAS EDWARD GREEN
born 26 June 1892,
admitted a pupil at Grasmere
Elementary School from
the Infants School, 1 May
1899, left 1 June 1906

FELIX BURNS GREEN
born 30 January 1895,
admitted a pupil at
Grasmere Elementary
School from the Infants
School, 29 April 1901,
left 14 May 1909

MARY
born 22 October
1890, admitted
a pupil at
Grasmere
Elementary School
from the Infants
School, 3 May 1891,
left 14 October 1904

AGNES
born 9 February
1906, admitted
a pupil at
Grasmere
Elementary School,
13 February 1911,
left 1 April 1920

28   A three-generation pedigree of the Green family between 1867 and 1920. This information was taken entirely from the Register of Admissions to Grasmere Elementary School

time at one of the two annual Hiring Fairs held in Kendal's market-place. By not having to pay rent the labourers hoped to be able to save enough from their wages to marry and take on a small farm of their own.

By 1861 John Green was working for Benson Harrison. Benson Harrison managed a Company called Harrison, Ainslie and Company, which ran an ironworks near Ulverston. Charcoal burning was an important process in producing this type of iron, and it is possible that John was leading two cartloads of charcoal for transportation down Windermere Lake to the ironworks when he was injured.

Benson Harrison also owned two blue slate quarries in Langdale. The Lakeland quarries provided roofing slates for most of northern England as well as for the walls of local buildings. John Green's grandson, James Green, lived in Grasmere and was a slate river when he married in 1890. A slate river's job was to split the hewn chunks of rock neatly down the cleavage plane ready for trimming to the required size and shape for use as building material. By 1895 James was a slate quarryman, which means that he helped to blast the rock from the working face, or hammered the rock into manageable lumps for the rivers to split. There were slate quarries at Elterwater, Coniston and Tilberthwaite as well as at Langdale, all close to Grasmere village where he lived. The gunpowder for blasting was provided by the gunpowder works at Elterwater.

From the middle of the nineteenth century, when the roads had been improved and extended, and the railway network stretched to Windermere, prosperous businessmen from places like Liverpool and Manchester began to have large country houses built for them to come and spend their summers in. Other rich people were attracted to the beauty and peacefulness of the Lake District and also settled there, especially in places like Grasmere and the surrounding area. This brought more employment for local people taken on as servants. It is possible that Thomas Green, father of James Green, and son of John, was engaged as a gardener at one or several such houses, tending the newly planted and landscaped gardens and trees.

Even though I can only suggest where the Greens might have worked, I was able to learn a lot about local life and industry in the nineteenth century from the local library in Windermere. The library has a collection of books on the history of the region, including the published writings of Dorothy Wordsworth, which told me more about George Green.

If you can discover a local Museum or library with a good collection of old photographs, these too can add to your knowledge of the working and living conditions of the period, as well as showing how local people looked and dressed.

In order to set up a trade a boy or girl would have to serve a term of apprenticeship first. This was usually over a period of seven or eight years, starting at the age of twelve or fourteen. Apprentices were normally housed, fed and clothed by their masters as well as being trained by them. The father or guardian of the child entered an agreement with the tradesman or craftsman and the details of their agreement were written down and signed by both parties. A copy was kept by each of them in case of any dispute. Apart from the years between 1710 and 1811, when the money paid for apprenticeship was taxed, it can be difficult to trace details of apprenticeship of an individual person, because they were personal documents and were usually destroyed once the period of training was completed. In boroughs and cities trade and industry were strictly regulated to make sure that there were not too many people competing with each other for business, and to control prices and to set standards of practice. Some of their records date from the Middle Ages. The Apprentice Binding Books tell you the name of the boy or girl, and of his father, the father's residence and occupation, the date and length of the apprenticeship and the sum paid for it, plus the name of the freeman agreeing to train the apprentice. The records of freemen contain names of apprentices who completed their service and were admitted, with the date. Some boroughs had guilds and Companies for individual trades. In the City of London there were many such companies. Their

RICHARD WORDSWORTH = MARY ROBINSON

of Sockbridge, Barton, Co.
Westmorland, buried
27 June 1760, at Barton,
M. I. there

married 25 May 1732,
at Lowther,
Co. Westmorland

RICHARD WORDSWORTH = ELIZABETH FAVELL

of Whitehaven, Co. Cumberland,
Collector of Customs, baptised
16 March 1732/3, at Lowther,
died 18 June 1794

died 1 March 1809

JOHN WORDSWORTH = ANN COOKSON

of Cockermouth
Co. Cumberland, attorney,
bap. 27 Nov 1741, at
Barton, died 30 Dec 1783

married 5 Feb 1766,
at Penrith St Andrew
Co. Cumberland, there
buried 11 March 1778,
aged 30

RICHARD WORDSWORTH = MARY SCOTT

of Branthwaite, Whitehaven,
attorney, bap. 23 Sept 1752,
at Normanton, Co. York

married 28 Feb 1775,
at Dean, Co. Cumberland

JOHN WORDSWORTH

of Penrith, Commander
of East Indiaman
Earl of Abergavenny
1789-95, bap. 16 April
1755, at Normanton,
died 22 and buried
25 Sept 1819 at Barton,
aged 64, M. I. there

Other issue

① RICHARD WORDSWORTH

② WILLIAM WORDSWORTH

④ CHRISTOPHER WORDSWORTH

Other issue

JOSEPH WORDSWORTH

3rd Mate on East Indiaman
Earl of Abergavenny, 1805,
bap. 18 Aug 1782, at Dean,
and 3 Dec 1782 at St Nicholas
Whitehaven

29   *A pedigree of the Wordsworth, Benson and Harrison families from 1728 to 1864. Note that Benson Harrison was given his mother's name at his baptism*

LEONARD BENSON = **AGNES BENSON**

of Skelwith, Hawkshead, Co. Lancaster, householder, buried 7 March 1738/9, at Hawkshead

married 28 April 1728, at Hawkshead, there buried 10 Feb 1739/40

Other issue

JOHN BENSON = **ELEANOR**

of Skelwith Fold, Hawkshead, bap. 26 Aug. 1731, at Hawkshead, there died 15, buried 19 Jan 1819. M. I.

died 28 Sept. 1805, aged 73, M. I. at Hawkshead

③

JOHN WORDSWORTH

Commander of East Indiaman Earl of Abergavenny, 1797-1805, born 4 Dec 1772, at Cockermouth, died 1 Feb 1805, on the Shambles off Portland Bill, Co. Dorset, buried at Lyme Regis, Co. Dorset

DOROTHY

born 25 Dec 1771, at Cockermouth, died 25 Jan 1855, at Rydal, Co. Westmorland buried 31 Jan 1855, at Grasmere, Co. Westmorland, aged 83, M. I. there

MATTHEW HARRISON = **MARY**

of Townson Ground, Coniston, Co. Lancaster, and Newland, Ulverston, Co. Lancaster, ironmaster, formerly steward to George Knott, and manager of Knott, Ainslie and Co., died 1 Nov 1824, aged 71, M. I. at Ulverston

bap. 22 June 1756, at Hawkshead, there married 24 Feb 1781, died 13 Jan 1839, aged 83, M. I. at Ulverston

Other issue

DOROTHY

of Scalehow, Ambleside, Co. Westmorland, 1864, bap. 30 Oct. 1800 at Dean, married 27 Sept 1823, at Green Bank, Ambleside 2nd wife

= **BENSON HARRISON** = **LOUISA LENNOX JOHNSON**

of The Lund, Green Bank, and Scalehow, all in Ambleside, magistrate and landowner, ironmaster, gunpowder manufacturer and shipowner (Harrison, Ainslie and Co.) at Newland, and at Bonaw, and Melfort, both Co. Argyle (Newland and Lorn Furnace Co.) born 12 Feb., bap. 29 March 1786, at Hawkshead, and 21 March 1789, at Ulverston, died 25 Nov 1863, at Water Park, Colton, Co. Lancaster, will dated 5 March 1859, proved with 7 codicils, 14 March 1864, M. I. at Ulverston

died 4 Jan 1820, aged 23, M. I. at Ulverston

1st wife

Other issue

He was one of the witnesses of William Wordsworth's will in 1847 and employed John Green records of apprenticeship bindings show that boys and girls came from all over the country to be apprenticed there.

You can sometimes find out what trade a person followed from the *Trade* and *Commercial Directories* described in Chapter 6. Local newspapers, besides carrying news, displayed advertisements paid for by local tradesmen offering their services and giving their addresses at the date of publication. Tradesmen were often itinerant, travelling round the country to find work. They took trade cards with them telling their customers where they could be found. Some of these cards still survive and there are good collections of them in the Guildhall Library in London and at the Bodleian Library in Oxford.

IMPORTANT NOTICE.

JOHN STRICKLAND AND SON,

BONE CRUSHERS AND MANURE MANUFACTURERS,

Ellerbeck Bone Works, Crook, near Kendal,

Are prepared to supply

Pure Raw Crushed ¼ inch Bones at £6   5s. per Ton.
Pure Raw Bone Meal at...   ...   £6 10s.   ,,
Their Noted Turnip Manure   ...   £6 0s.   ,,
Excellent Manure for Top Dressing
  Corn and Grass...   ...   ...   £4 10s.   ,,
  The above Prices are delivered at the Works, Kendal, or Staveley Station.   Time of Payment, October 24th, 1891.   Discount of 5/- per Ton allowed on Cash Payments.

FURTHER NOTICE.

  JOHN STRICKLAND & SON will give £5 5s. in Four Money Prizes, viz., First, £2; Second, £1 10s.; Third, £1; Fourth, 15s., to the Competitors who will shew to the Inspectors of the Crosthwaite and Underbarrow Agricultural Society, Two Acres each of Swede Turnips grown with One Ton of Turnip Manure purchased from them.

Lice on Cattle.

IT may be scarcely necessary to remind Farmers of the danger of using Sheep Dips as Cattle Washes, especially some of the so-called "NON-POISONOUS" ones.   Not long ago, they may remember, was recorded in our local Papers a lamentable instance of this kind of folly, resulting as it did in the death of several Cattle.

GREAVES' **L**ICE **P**ASTE

Is a perfectly safe and most effective cure for these pests, leaving the skin of the beast clean, the hair soft and silky, and generally improving its appearance.

  Price One Shilling per lb., One Pound making One Gallon of Wash.

Prepared and Sold only by

H I N D, Chemist, Kendal.

CUMBRIA RECORD OFFICE

30   *Extract from the advertisements in the* Westmorland Gazette *for 14 March 1891, the week when John Green's death was reported*

Local traders and craftsmen often formed themselves into Friendly Societies. Members paid a fixed weekly or monthly sum into a central fund. This fund was used to give financial help to members and their families who fell on hard times and were not able to support themselves. From 1793 the rules and regulations of Friendly Societies had to be filed at a meeting of the local justices, which was held four times a year and was called the County Quarter Sessions. The records of the Quarter Sessions are held in County Record Offices and occasionally date back to the sixteenth century. They deal with administrative and judicial affairs in the county, but as the documents are very bulky they have often not been sorted or catalogued and are difficult to search. Among the papers of the Quarter Sessions are the annual licences granted to certain types of traders, for instance victuallers, corn dealers, butchers and printers.

Later on in the century, with the growth of industry, groups of workers began to form Unions. Their organization covered the whole country and local branches sprang up. Some Unions still hold their own lists of members, but many have been deposited at the Modern Records Centre at the University of Warwick, at Coventry. Union records can be used to trace a man's age at joining, his places of work, home addresses and Union activities.

Other records about tradesmen include their business accounts, detailing their day-to-day expenses and payments of wages and bills, and insurance policies which they took out to protect themselves against the cost of repairs if their premises caught fire. People began to insure their homes and businesses against fire from the late seventeenth century, but most Assurance Societies were set up in the eighteenth century or later. A local *Directory* of the time will tell you which Societies served your area when your ancestor was there. The Societies filed details of the premises insured, the value and type of stock held on them, the name of their owner, and the sum paid for insurance. Most of these records are still held by the Societies and it is best to write to them if you want to know about a person at a specific date, because many of the policies remain unsorted.

Sometimes a new technique of production was invented or discovered. The inventor could protect his interests by applying for a patent to the Patent Office in London. Before 1852 the patents were enrolled on the Patent Rolls, now in the Public Record Office in London. Later ones are at the Patent Office. There is a printed index of names of patentees since 1617 so that you can easily discover whether one of your family ever took out a patent, at what date, and in what field.

IMMIGRANT ANCESTORS

If one of your ancestors was an immigrant worker, there are a variety of ways in which you can try to trace where he came from. If the family came to this country within living memory, obviously it is best to ask them for information and for any family and official papers they may have kept which will tell you when and where they came from. This is because our public records often only reveal a person's country of origin, which is rarely enough to be of much help. You may even discover that the family is still in contact with relatives who stayed behind.

Another way of finding a person's date and place of birth abroad is by finding him in the Census Returns, although usually only the country of birth is disclosed.

Lists of ships' passengers coming here from abroad survive only from 1878, and these do not relate to people arriving from Europe or from ports on the Mediterranean

Sea. Ages, occupations and addresses of passengers in this country are all that are given, together with their date of arrival. Aliens arriving before this, or whose names cannot be found in the passenger lists, may be located in the Denization and Naturalization papers, held, like the ships' passenger lists, at the Public Record Office at Kew. There are typescript indices of people who were naturalized as British citizens, or who obtained partial citizenship (denization) from 1509 until 1924, to help you to identify an applicant. As mentioned in Chapter 4, the original application papers provide background information about birth, marriage, and the person's immediate family, and sometimes state the reason for coming to Britain. These are a valuable source if you are lucky enough to find your ancestor among the papers.

Large numbers of refugees came to England from France after the Revocation of the Edict of Nantes in 1685, and the French Revolution in 1789. Letters and papers concerning many of them are also in the Public Record Office at Kew. Names of people who applied to and received money from special public funds can also be found among these documents, and details of their circumstances are often attached to their claims for help.

From 1792 onwards, immigration was strictly controlled because of the wars with France. Aliens had to register their names, lodgings and occupations with the County Quarter Sessions. After the Aliens Act of 1836, certificates of arrival were filed of all newcomers disembarking at each port in the United Kingdom. Their names, nationalities, occupations and dates of arrival were written down, and you can examine these at the Public Record Office at Kew.

Once here, immigrants tended to cluster around the ports of entry. The Huguenot Society has published all the records of baptism, marriage and burial from the foreign Protestant churches set up here. These sometimes give clues as to places of origin, but usually families established themselves in the community fairly quickly and perhaps the only indication that a person was an immigrant may come from his will which mentioned people and places abroad.

Book List
J.S.W. Gibson   *Quarter Sessions Records for Family Historians: a select list* 1982
J.C. and L.L. Neagles   *Locating your Immigrant Ancestor, A Guide to Naturalization Records* 1974

CHAPTER EIGHT
Records of the Professions: the Wordsworths

AFTER THE WORDSWORTH family left Grasmere in 1813, they went to live at Rydal Mount nearby. Dorothy Wordsworth was there at the time of the 1841 and 1851 Censuses. In 1851 she was aged 79, and her sister-in-law, Mary Wordsworth, was a widow of 80. Dorothy died in 1855 and was buried at Grasmere, close to her brother William, and there are gravestones to both of them in the churchyard there.

The letters and other family papers which they left behind have been much studied and written about. From these it is possible to build up a picture of how they lived and thought. I shall now use the Wordsworth family to illustrate how you can trace ancestors who were well educated, entered the professions, were commissioned in the Armed Services, or travelled abroad to seek a career.

Because William Wordsworth was a famous poet, I looked first for an entry about him in the *Dictionary of National Biography*. This contained a brief outline of his life and writings and referred me to other books and articles where I could learn more about him. The *Dictionary* told me that he was born at Cockermouth in Cumberland on 7th April 1770, and that he was educated there and at Penrith, before entering Hawkshead Grammar School with his older brother Richard in 1778.

UNIVERSITY RECORDS
The nobility and landed classes generally sent their sons to university after school. Cambridge and Oxford were the only universities in England until the early nineteenth century, but sometimes students were sent to one of the four Scottish universities or to a Continental university to study Science or Medicine. Many of the new middle class, whose wealth was based on industry, did not belong to the

Near the Graves of two young Children
removed from a Family to which through life she was devoted
HERE LIES THE BODY
OF
SARAH HUTCHINSON,
The beloved Sister and faithful Friend
Mourners who have caused this Stone to be erected
with an earnest wish that their own Remains
may be laid by her side, and a humble hope
that, through Christ, they may together
made Partakers of the same blessed Resurrection
SHE WAS BORN AT PENRITH 1ST JANY 1775,
AND DIED AT RYDAL 23RD JUNE 1835.
In Fulfilment of that Wish,
are now gathered near her the Remains of
WILLIAM WORDSWORTH,
Born at Cockermouth 7th April 1770,
Died at Rydal 23rd April 1850;
And of
DOROTHY WORDSWORTH,
Born at Cockermouth 25th December 1771,
Died at Rydal 25th January 1855;
And finally of
MARY WORDSWORTH,
Wife of WILLIAM WORDSWORTH,
and Sister of SARAH HUTCHINSON:
Born at Penrith, August 16th, 1770;
Died at Rydal Mount, January 17th, 1859.

Church of England and their sons were therefore not admitted to Oxford or Cambridge until the mid-nineteenth century. The curricula offered by the universities abroad were often much more modern and technical than the English.

Registers of Admissions of students have been published in a few cases, but it is best to write to the University Registrar for details of a particular student's career, because University records often contain much more information than ever appears in print. The printed *Alumni Cantabrigienses*, being a record of all students at the University of Cambridge until 1900 with details of their family background and subsequent careers where known, shows that William Wordsworth was admitted to St John's College Cambridge in October 1787, and that he received his degree in January 1791. According to family letters, his uncle was already a Fellow of the College, and his cousin was a student there. William sent his own son, John, to St John's College in 1821. Families often had a traditional connexion with a particular College and sent several generations to it.

THE PROFESSIONS

It was the custom for sons of wealthier families to enter one of the professions, such as the law or the church, or to have a commission purchased in the Army or Royal Navy. Most professions have organized themselves into Associations or Societies setting strict standards for admission. *Whitaker's Almanack* contains a list of such bodies and their addresses and dates of formation. From their Lists and Directories you can often uncover clues as to where a person was at a certain date, when and where he qualified and approximately when he ceased to practise.

THE LAW

William Wordsworth went to university with the intention of becoming a lawyer like his father, grandfather, uncle, cousin and brother before him, but this did not come about. To be a lawyer he would have had to be articled as a clerk to a practising attorney for five years, and once he completed the term successfully he would have sought admission to the Courts to practise. The filed Indentures of the articles of clerkship from 1729 are now in the Public Record Office in London. There are indices to them. The Indentures record the names of the attorney and his clerk, and the name and address of the clerk's parent or guardian. From 1775 annually published *Law Lists* began to appear. They contain the names and addresses of all practising attorneys in London and the provinces. The Law Society, which was

31 (opposite)   The monumental inscription of Wordsworth and his family in Grasmere churchyard. This is a very helpful inscription, because it gives dates of birth and death, and family relationships ALAN NEVINSON

JOHN CHRISTIAN = **BRIDGET SENHOUSE**

died 25 Sept 1745 at Dearham, Co. Cumberland

married 14 May 1717, at Ellenborough, Co. Cumberland, died 27 Sept 1749, at Dearham

CHARLES CHRISTIAN = **ANN DIXON**

of Morland Close, Cockermouth, Co. Cumberland, attorney, born 12 Dec 1729, at Dearham, died 11 March 1768, aged 38, M.I. at Brigham, Co. Cumberland

married 2 May 1751, at Brigham

JOHN WORDSWORTH = **ANN COOKSON**

of Cockermouth, attorney, bap. 27 Nov 1741, at Barton, Co. Westmorland, died 20 Dec 1783

married 5 Feb 1766 at St Andrew Penrith, Co. Cumberland, there buried 11 March 1778, aged 30

Other issue

FLETCHER CHRISTIAN

Master's Mate and acting Lieutenant on H.M.S. Bounty, 1787-28 April 1789, one of the mutineers, bap. 25 Sept 1764 at Brigham

Other issue

① RICHARD WORDSWORTH = **JANE WESTMORLAND**

of Sockbridge, Barton, and Staple Inn, London, Co. Middlesex, attorney, held land at Cockermouth, Brigham, Ravenglass, Co. Cumberland, and Clifton, Co. Westmorland, born 19 August 1768, at Cockermouth, died 19 May 1816, in London, will dated 6 May 1816, proved 24 April 1817

married 9 Feb 1814 at Addingham, Co. Cumberland

② WILLIAM WORDSWORTH

of Dove Cottage, Allan Bank, and Parsonage, Grasmere, Co. Westmorland, and Rydal Mount, Co. Westmorland, Distributor of Stamps for Westmorland 1813-42, Poet Laureate 1843-50, born 7 April 1770, at Cockermouth, Bachelor of Arts of the University of Cambridge (St John's College), died 23 April 1850 at Rydal Mount, buried 27 April 1850, at Grasmere, M.I. there, will dated 31 Aug 1847, proved with codicil 27 May 1850

= **MARY HUTCHINSON**

born 16 Aug 1770, at Penrith, married 4 Oct 1802, at Brompton, Co. York, died 17 Jan 1859, at Rydal Mount, buried 21 Jan 1859, at Grasmere, M.I. there

DOROTHY

born 25 Dec 1771, at Cockermouth, died 25 Jan 1855, at Rydal Mount, buried 31 Jan 1855 at Grasmere, aged 83, M.I. there

JOHN WORDSWORTH

Member of the Royal College of Surgeons (England), Staff Assistant Surgeon in H.M. Army Medical Service in the Ionian Islands, bap. 4 March 1815, at Barton, died 18 August 1846, at Ambleside, Co. Westmorland, buried 22 August 1846, at Grasmere, M.I. there

Other issue   **JOHN WORDSWORTH** = **ISABELLA CHRISTIA**

Clerk in Holy Orders, Rector of Moresby, 1829-34, of Workington 1834-40, and of Plumbland, 1840-75, all in Co. Cumberland, born 18 June, bap. 17 July 1803, at Grasmere, Bachelor of Arts of the University of Oxford (New College), ordained a priest, 1828, died 25 July 1875, at Bruton Street, Eaton Square, London, Co. Middlesex, will dated 20 Oct 1871, proved 13 Nov 1875

married 11 Oct 1830 a St Michael Workingto

1st wife

32   Pedigree of the Wordsworth, Christian and Curwen families from 1717 to 1875.

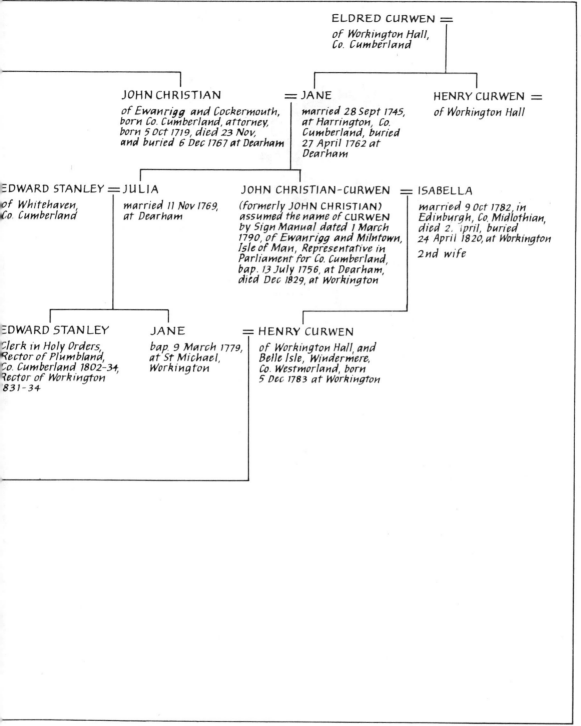

ELDRED CURWEN =
*of Workington Hall,
Co. Cumberland*

JOHN CHRISTIAN   = JANE   HENRY CURWEN =
of Ewanrigg and Cockermouth,   *married 28 Sept 1745,*   *of Workington Hall*
born Co. Cumberland, attorney,   *at Harrington, Co.*
born 5 Oct 1719, died 23 Nov,   *Cumberland, buried*
and buried 6 Dec 1767 at Dearham   *27 April 1762 at*
Dearham

EDWARD STANLEY = JULIA   JOHN CHRISTIAN-CURWEN = ISABELLA
of Whitehaven,   *married 11 Nov 1769,*   *(formerly JOHN CHRISTIAN)*   *married 9 Oct 1782, in*
Co. Cumberland   *at Dearham*   *assumed the name of CURWEN*   *Edinburgh, Co. Midlothian,*
     by Sign Manual dated 1 March   *died 2. April, buried*
     1790, of Ewanrigg and Milntown,   *24 April 1820, at Workington*
     Isle of Man, Representative in   *2nd wife*
     Parliament for Co. Cumberland,
     bap. 13 July 1756, at Dearham,
     died Dec 1829, at Workington

EDWARD STANLEY   JANE   = HENRY CURWEN
Clerk in Holy Orders,   *bap. 9 March 1779,*   *of Workington Hall, and*
Rector of Plumbland,   *at St Michael,*   *Belle Isle, Windermere,*
Co. Cumberland 1802–34,   *Workington*   *Co. Westmorland, born*
Rector of Workington   *5 Dec 1783 at Workington*
1831–34

*Fletcher Christian, one of the mutineers on HMS Bounty in 1789,
was a contemporary of the Wordsworths at Cockermouth*

incorporated in 1832, and the Society of Genealogists in London, have good collections of *Law Lists.*

BY PERMISSION OF THE TRUSTEES OF DOVE COTTAGE
33   Portrait of William Wordsworth by Edridge, 1805

Barristers underwent training in one of the Inns of Court. Registers of Admissions to the Inns date back to the Middle Ages. They often give a student's parentage and place of abode at the time of entry to the Inn. A few of these Registers have been copied and printed, but the bulk of them are uncopied and are held by the various Inns.

THE CHURCH

Sometimes a wealthy or landed family had the right to nominate the incumbent of a living. The nomination was subject to the Bishop's approval. The incumbent was given a house to live in and a piece of land, called the glebe. He could cultivate the glebeland for his own use or let it out to tenants and charge them rent. The house and lands were often extensive, as they were provided by the patron nominating the incumbent, who was often a relative. At Grasmere the patrons were the Le Fleming family of Rydal Hall, and several Le Flemings were Rectors there.

BY PERMISSION OF THE TRUSTEES OF DOVE COTTAGE

34   Portrait of the Reverend John Wordsworth, the poet's son. This portrait hangs in the vestry at Moresby church, where he was rector between 1829 and 1834

Printed *Clergy Lists* of ordained Anglican clergymen in England and overseas first began to appear regularly from 1836. They merely listed each clergyman's name and address with the name of the patron of his living and the income derived from it. From 1858, and almost every year thereafter, Crockford's *Clerical Directory* was published. This contains fuller information, including where the clergyman trained, when and where he was ordained and his career to date. Once you have found where he was ordained, a search of the Ordination papers (held in Diocesan Registries or County Record Offices) should reveal not only testimonials and letters of recommendation from the ordinand's College and parson, but frequently also his baptism certificate, showing when and where he was baptized, and the names of both his parents. When a clergyman's name disappears from the *Directory* it is a good idea to start looking for his death certificate, for a memorial to him in the church or churchyard where he was last incumbent, and for his obituary in the parish magazine and local newspaper.

THE MEDICAL PROFESSION

The other profession which attracted students was Medicine. *Medical Registers* and annual *Medical Directories* did not start to be published until the 1830s. They contain information about the training, careers and present addresses of all medical practitioners in Great Britain at the time of going to press. At the back of each volume is a section devoted to death notices and obituaries of doctors who have died during the previous year. Because they were so important to the community it is always worth looking in the local newspaper for a more detailed obituary once you know when a doctor died.

Until the nineteenth century surgeons were considered socially inferior to physicians. They were often barbers as well. In the Guildhall Library in London are the records of the Barber Surgeons Company of the City of London. They date from the sixteenth century and include apprenticeship binding books and registers of freemen showing when and whence a person came up to London to train, and when he was admitted to the Company.

When the Royal College of Surgeons of England was founded in 1800, surgery became more acceptable as a profession, and its members and Fellows were elected. Surgeons began to be trained at University Medical Schools and at teaching hospitals. Although surgeons had been held in low esteem in England, the Royal College of Surgeons of Edinburgh, founded in 1505, and the Medical Schools of the Universities of Edinburgh, Glasgow and Dublin had international reputations long before the nineteenth century and had drawn students from England. It is worth writing to the Registrars of these Schools if an ancestor trained there because their Admission Registers contain useful information about the origin and subsequent career of students.

Potted biographies have been published of physicians elected members and Fellows of the Royal College of Physicians of London since its foundation in 1518 and before 1925. There are also printed lists of members and Fellows of the Royal

Sacred to the Memory of
JOHN WORDSWORTH,
STAFF ASSISTANT SURGEON
TO HER MAJESTY'S FORCES
IN THE IONIAN ISLANDS,
ONLY SON OF THE LATE
RICHARD WORDSWORTH,
OF SOCKBRIDGE, IN THIS COUNTY,
AND NEPHEW OF
WILLIAM WORDSWORTH,
OF RYDAL MOUNT
HE DIED AT AMBLESIDE
ON THE 18TH DAY OF AUGUST, 1846,
AGED 31 YEARS, MUCH LAMENTED.

JACK LOAN

35   The gravestone of the poet's nephew John Wordsworth, who died at Ambleside but was buried at Grasmere on 22 August 1846, aged 31. The inscription tells us that he was an army surgeon and had served abroad, information which might otherwise have been very difficult to obtain

College of Physicians of Edinburgh from 1681, and of the Royal College of Physicians and Surgeons of Glasgow from 1599.

THE BRITISH ARMY

Until 1755 Britain had no national standing Army. The Regiments were called guards and garrisons, and were raised to meet special needs. They took the names of their Colonels until 1756, when a numbering system was introduced. There were cavalry, infantry, artillery and engineer Regiments, and each was composed of several companies under the command of captains (the cavalry was made up of troops instead of companies). Until 1870, officers' commissions were almost always by purchase except in special circumstances and in the artillery and engineer regiments. This meant that the upper classes dominated the ranks of officers. The lower ranks were recruited from boys aged eighteen and upwards, although this rule was not strictly observed. Few made the Army a lifelong career – many were discharged after war service, or were wounded or killed, or bought their freedom. Military records up to 1913 are now at the Public Record Office at Kew, while later ones are held by the Army Records Centre at Hayes.

William Wordsworth's grandson, John Wordsworth, served in the 77th (East Middlesex) Regiment of Foot between 1855 and 1869. From the printed *Army Lists* of officers which started to appear each year from 1754 I learned that he was commissioned in the Regiment as an Ensign on 8th November 1855. Later *Lists* showed that he purchased a commission as Lieutenant on 4th March 1859, and rose to the rank of Captain on 1st July 1867.

The Commander-in-Chief's Memoranda, beginning in 1793, contain officers' retirements, resignations and applications for commissions.

On 6th July 1855 John Wordsworth's father, the Reverend John Wordsworth, wrote from Brigham Vicarage in Cumberland to the War Office on his son's behalf. He said that while his son had failed his Latin and French examinations, 'This is easily accounted for since till lately he had laid aside attending to those languages intending to go out to the Colonies.' He went on: 'As another journey hence to Sandhurst is attended with considerable expense perhaps you would kindly allow my son to pass without doing so, as I undertake whilst he remains here to work him well in his Latin & he has an opp[y] here of being put under good instruction in the french Language.' Not surprisingly, the War Office declined to bend their rules in John's favour, but he was allowed to apply to take the Latin and French examinations again as soon as he felt ready. Apparently he succeeded at his second attempt, for by mid-1856 he was at the Regimental Depot on the Isle of Wight. In June 1857 he set sail for Sydney in Australia, and during his service he was also stationed at various places in the East Indies until he returned to England in March 1868.

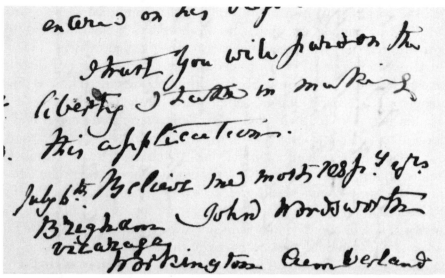

36 *Part of the Reverend John Wordsworth's optimistic letter to the War Office, 6 July 1855:* WO 31 1102

allow my son to pass without doing so, as I undertake whilst he remains here to work him well in his Latin & he has an opp[y] here of being put under good instruction in the french Language. Mr Browne, with whom he has been for two months speaks most favorably (*sic*) of his good conduct & industry, & I am convinced it is his present resolution to do his very best, in every way, to be a credit to the military profession. Of course, if this favor (*sic*) cannot be granted my son must present himself again at Sandhurst in the course of another 6 weeks or 2 months.

The favor (*sic*) however, I ask, I should esteem a great one if it could be granted, as I have four sons just now to put forward in life on our income of some £600 per an. My second son has just entered on his Oxford career.

I trust you will pardon the liberty I take in making this application.

Believe me most resp[y] yrs

JOHN WORDSWORTH

July 6th, Brigham Vicarage, Workington, Cumberland

His travels were traced through the monthly and quarterly Muster Rolls of the Regiment. The Musters, or roll calls of personnel, record the names of every serving man in the Regiment at the time they were taken, arranged by rank and then alphabetically by surname. The Muster for December 1869 noted that Captain John Wordsworth had retired on 14th December. Another look at the Commander-in-Chief's Memoranda for that month yielded a good deal of information about John Wordsworth, though of a somewhat negative kind. He was examined by the Staff Surgeon on 3rd September 1869 and was found to be in a good state of health. A grant of £1450 was paid to him on the sale of his commission. His statement of services, in the Memoranda, show that he was born at Brigham on 23rd July 1837, and that he entered the Army aged eighteen years and five months. He fought no battles, sustained no wounds, won no medals, his conduct was not distinguished, nor did he earn any situations on the Staff. At the time he retired he was unmarried.

Other sources for tracing officers' origins are the signed Returns of Officers' Services which began in 1828. In this year all officers retired on full and half pay were recorded together with details of their career in the Army, their age at commission, date and place of marriage and children's births. From 1829, the Returns relate only to officers on active service and contain their date and place of birth. There is a fairly complete slip index to these Returns in the Public Record Office at Kew. Widows' pension applications made between 1755 and 1908 also contain personal details about dead officers and their families, such as their marriage certificates, and the date and circumstances of their demise.

Other ranks can be difficult to trace before 1883, unless they were discharged to pension. This is because all the other records of attestation and discharge were destroyed. The surviving papers are arranged by Regiment and then alphabetically by surname, and relate to soldiers who were pensioned off after 1756. Their ages at enlistment, birthplaces and occupation or trade outside the Army are recorded, with details of Army service, medical and conduct reports and the dates and places of discharge. There is also a description of the soldier's physical appearance which will tell you about his height, build, colouring and any disfiguring marks. From 1854 the pensioners' intended abodes were added, and from 1883 the names of the next of kin. After 1883, too, the Attestation and Discharge papers survive for all serving men and are arranged alphabetically by surname, regardless of Regiment, which makes searching easier.

If you do not know the name of the Regiment to which a soldier belonged, sometimes his marriage certificate or the birth certificate of one of his offspring will help to identify it. You should look at the indices of the Regimental Returns at the General Register Office for a reference to his name after 1761. I have described what the Returns contain in Chapter 2. If you know where a man was at a particular date a search of the Station Returns will tell you which Regiments were stationed there at the time. Even a photograph of a soldier in uniform may be enough for the Regiment to be identified by the National Army Museum in London and it is always worth approaching the Museum for advice. Having found the number of the Regiment you should then search the appropriate Attestation and Discharge papers for the man's name. If you still fail to find him, then you could try the Muster Rolls described earlier in this chapter. In the ranks of soldiers recorded each month their dates of enlistment were stated. If you then look at the Muster covering this date you can discover his age at enlistment. You should then trace his name through the Musters

Bounty Paid	Nº	Entry.	Year	Appearance.	Whence and whether Prest or not.	Place and County where Born.	Age at Time of Entry in this Ship	Nº and Letter of Tickets	MEN'S NAMES.	Qualities	D. D.D. or R.	Time of Discharge
	11	27 Aug	1787	Aug 27	Volr	Hanover	24		Henry Hilbrant	Ab	R	28 April
	14	" "	"	" "	"	Orkneys	21		George Stewart	Mid Ab	R	
	15	" "	"	" "	"	Douglas Isle of Man	15		Peter Heywood	Ab	R	28 "
	19	29 "	"	" 29	"	Sunderland	23		John Charlton	Ab	R	27 Novr
	20	" "	"	" "	"	Hadley Suffolk	20		John Cooper	Ab	R	7 Sept
	20	30 "	—	" 31	"	Whitehaven	35		Geo: Armstrong	Ab	R	28 "
		" "	"	" "	"	Philidelphia	30		Isaac Martin	Ab	Rn	28 April
		" "	"	" "	"	Whitehaven	26		Willm Hudson	Ab	R	7 Octr
	24	" "	"	" "	"	Sunderland	25		John Sican	ill	R	27 Nor
	26	7 Sept	"	Sept 7	"	Manchester	20		Charles Churchill	Corp l	R	
		" "	"	" "	"	Tunbridge Wells	22		Richd Skinner	Ab	R	28 April
		" "	"	" "	"	Hull	20		Saml Sutton	Ab	R	7 Octr
	29	" "	"	" "	"	London	20		Alexr Smith	Ab	R	28 April
	31	" "	"	" "	"	Whitehaven	21		Fletcher Christian	Mastersmate	R	28 "
		" "	"	" "	"	London	27		James Kainey	Ab	R	12 Sept
		" "	"	" "	"	Bath	21		Thomas Burkitt	Ab	R	

37   Part of the list of deserters in the muster (crew list) of HMS Bounty, 1789. Fletcher Christian, one of the leaders of the mutiny on 28 April 1789, was the master's mate on board ship. At the time he joined ship in 1787 he gave his age as 21 and his birthplace as Whitehaven. These lists are useful because they give both approximate dates of birth and birthplaces. ADM 36/10744 Crown copyright

until it disappears. Find the list of Non-Effectives (soldiers no longer active in the regiment) for the quarter of the year in which he has disappeared, and this should reveal the date and reason for discharge and his birthplace and civilian occupation.

THE ROYAL NAVY

As continuous engagement of ordinary seamen did not start until 1853 it is difficult to follow a sailor's career if it ended before this, as he was taken on for individual voyages and then discharged. Crew lists or Musters of Royal Naval vessels from 1667 are held in the Public Record Office at Kew, along with other naval material. The Musters were taken at regular intervals, usually every six months, and listed each man's name, rank, date of joining the ship, whether he had been impressed to join or had volunteered, and the date and reason for his discharge. From about 1770 age at entering the vessel and birthplaces were added. If you do not know the name of a ship in which your ancestor served, but you know where he was at a specific date, the Naval List Books, starting in 1673, will tell you which ships were there then and you can search the Ships' Musters for his name. From 1853 the Continuous Engagement Books record the dates and places of birth and naval service of all seamen active at that time and afterwards. The Books are indexed.

Sailors wounded on active service were entitled to receive a pension from the Chatham Chest. This fund was begun in 1617 and closed in 1807. It was made up of monthly deductions taken from every seaman's pay. The registers of payments made out of the fund include among the application papers details of how the injuries were sustained and the sailor's present circumstances. There are indices to these for the years between 1744 and 1797. Seamen who became inmates of Greenwich Hospital after 1737 are recorded in the Hospital Registers, with their dates of death or discharge. As their families often stayed with them, it is worth looking at the Greenwich Hospital School Registers for entries of their children's names. Mothers, widows and orphans of sailors killed at sea could apply to the Bounty Office for relief. Their application papers, ranging between 1675 and 1822, include marriage, birth and death certificates and other personal family information forwarded by the claimants. There is a typescript index to dead seamen on whose behalf claims were made.

There were two types of Royal Naval officer, those commissioned by the Crown (including Admirals, Captains, Commanders and Lieutenants), and those given warrants by the Captains because of their skills (like the master, boatswain, gunner, engineer, carpenter, surgeon and midshipman). The best record of commissioned and warrant officers' careers is the series of Returns of Services dating from the late eighteenth century and relating to careers which had often begun much earlier.

Annual *Navy Lists* of commissioned officers began to appear annually from 1782,

NATIONAL MARITIME MUSEUM

38   An aquatint by R. Dodd, showing the mutineers on HMS Bounty turning Lieut. Bligh and some of the officers and crew adrift Negative number B. 1337

and there is also a printed *List of Commissioned Sea Officers 1660–1815* which will tell you when an officer was promoted. From 1691, intending Lieutenants were required to be examined by the Admiralty as to their suitability for promotion. Their passing certificates, and those issued by the Navy Board from 1731 to Lieutenants, boatswains, pursers and gunners, detail the number of years, months, weeks and days a candidate had served on each vessel, and at what rank. From about the last quarter of the eighteenth century baptism certificates were attached, but these are not always reliable because certificates were sometimes forged to show that candidates were over the age of twenty-one as required by the examiners.

Warrant Books, dating from the early eighteenth century, only record the date when an officer received his warrant, the name of ship and the Captain issuing it, and his previous rank, so that they are not much use to the family historian seeking to discover his age and birthplace.

If you want to find out about conditions on board ship, and where it sailed, the Ships' Logs are worth reading. These date from about 1688.

Records about the Royal Marines start in 1790, and contain the same biographical information as the Army Attestation and Discharge papers. They are arranged under year of discharge until 1883 and then by year of enlistment. Details of officers' services survive from 1793, but are not complete before 1837 because short periods of service were omitted. The Returns often give the names of the fathers of the officers.

THE MERCHANT NAVY

Men who were seamen engaged in merchant trade can usually only be traced before 1835 in the Crew Lists of the ships in which they sailed. From 1747 masters or shipowners were obliged to keep a muster of crewmen on each voyage, giving their names, abodes and dates of enlistment, and the name of their previous vessel. Few such lists survive, but those which do are in the Public Record Office at Kew, among the papers relating to the Board of Trade.

From 1835 until 1856 there was a system of compulsory registration of merchant seamen. After 1844 the registers were organized by ticket numbers, but there are indices to them, listing the names and ports of registration, and ticket numbers of mercantile mariners. The tickets record a seaman's name, physical appearance, date and place of birth, age at first going to sea and at what rank, his rank at the time of ticketing, his normal place of abode when not at sea, and his ability to read and write. Compulsory certificates of competence began to be issued to other categories of merchant seamen, like masters and mates, from 1854, engineers from 1862, and skippers and mates of fishing vessels from 1883, and all of these record dates and places of birth and previous naval service. After 1856 merchant seamen can generally only be traced via the Crew Lists, but relatively few are preserved at the Public Record Office at Kew, the rest being widely dispersed.

The printed *Mercantile Navy Lists*, starting in 1857, record the names of all officers in the Merchant Service with their dates of seniority, so that you can discover a man's dates of promotion.

A wounded merchant seaman, or one rendered unfit for further service, and who was unable to support himself and his family, was not given a pension. Instead, he had to apply to Trinity House for relief. Petitions made by merchant mariners or their widows survive for the years between 1780 and 1854, and are held by the Society of Genealogists in London. They are organized alphabetically under the name of each claimant, and attached to the petitions is supporting evidence like marriage and baptism certificates, testimonials from the mariner's last employer and parish priest, and they record the cause of his misfortune, his present place of residence and his signature or mark.

THE BRITISH ABROAD

Unfortunately there is no regular series of ships' passenger lists of people travelling overseas before 1890, apart from sporadic seventeenth century lists, most of which have now been published. The later lists are arranged by port of departure and then by date of sailing. They give the place of destination, age and occupation of every passenger on board according to his class of ticket. Failing this, it is a matter of finding out what records there are relating to people on arrival at the other end, which might reveal where they came from.

In some cases, particularly in India, connexions with the home country were always very strong. Some records of people in India were sent back to this country and can be searched in the India Office Library in London.

The Honourable British East India Company was founded in 1600 to do trade with India. The Company divided the country into three administrative units, the Presidencies of Bengal, Bombay, and Madras. Each kept its own records of baptism, marriage and burial, and registers of wills. The Company's officers controlled trading to such an extent that they virtually governed the country and up until 1834 anyone wishing to trade in India had to apply to the Company for a licence. These

BY PERMISSION OF THE BRITISH LIBRARY

39   *Bombay on the Malabar coast: an engraving by Jan van Ryne, 1794. This is how Bombay looked at the time of John Wordsworth's voyages to India Library no. P.15 Negative no. B.2513*

applications are held by the India Office Library. Records of Britons wishing to be employed by the Company as civil servants after 1749 are also deposited there. Birth certificates and testimonials from friends and relations are included among the papers.

Ship embarkation lists of passengers sailing to India date from 1753, and are also at the India Office Library. These are useful because they give names, ages, status and place of origin and destination of everyone who travelled there.

From 1803 printed *Directories* and *Almanacks* of the East Indies supply names and addresses of Company officials and private residents in India, and there is a good collection of these volumes at the India Office Library.

Returns of British births, baptisms, marriage and burials, made by the Anglican chaplains in India, can also be seen at the India Office Library. The earliest, covering the Presidency of Madras, begins in 1698. The Returns are incomplete because some of the original registers were destroyed or lost, but sometimes gaps in the Returns can be made up by consulting entries in Indian newspapers of the day. The Society of Genealogists in London has typed indices to many such entries. You could also try searching *The Times* for birth, marriage and death announcements of the British in India, although they were often not reported in this country until some months afterwards. Copies of many of the gravestone inscriptions to Britons who died in India, and the registers of wills of people leaving property there from the early eighteenth century onwards, can be searched at the India Office Library.

The Honourable East India Company also had its own Army, Navy and Merchant Navy. Cadet papers relating to those men who wished to be commissioned as officers in one of the Company's Regiments between 1789 and 1860 have filed with them the birth certificates of applicants, and letters of introduction from relatives and friends. Commission papers of officers in the Indian Navy contain similar information. There are also Musters of Army and Navy personnel to help you to locate a person at a specific date.

William Wordsworth's brother John was employed in the Indian Merchant Navy. He first sailed as a midshipman from England to Bombay and Canton in China on board the East Indiaman *Earl of Abergavenny* at the end of January 1790. His cousin, John Wordsworth, was the ship's commander. Altogether William's brother made four voyages to India, and rose to be Commander. From Marine Records at the India Office Library I discovered that he was baptized at St Mary's Church, Cockermouth, Cumberland, on 4th December 1773, the son of John and Ann Wordsworth. He went to sea in 1788. His first voyage to Bombay and China took a year and ten months and on 29th September 1791 he was paid £23 2s 11d for his services on board ship, according to the Pay Books. His wages as midshipman were based on twenty-six shillings a month, from which certain deductions were made. Later on, as Commander, he received £10 a month. John's final voyage was intended to be to

BY PERMISSION OF THE BRITISH LIBRARY

40   The Earl of Abergavenny, *East Indiaman, off Southsea. A painting by Thomas Luny, 1801. When this ship was wrecked off Portland Bill in 1805, many of the passengers and crew were drowned and cargo to the value of £200,000 was lost. John Wordsworth, the Commander, was among the victims*
Library no. F.59

Bengal to load up with cotton for the China market. The *Earl of Abergavenny* left Portsmouth on 1st February 1805, but was lost on the Shambles off Portland Bill, in Dorset, four days later, when the ship struck a rock. More than four hundred passengers and soldiers were on board, and almost three-quarters of them were drowned, including the commander, Captain Wordsworth. His cousin, Joseph Wordsworth, the third mate, was one of the survivors.

Often travel abroad was not meant to be permanent, but merely to establish a trading base. Traders and planters in the West Indies can be traced in records in the United Kingdom. For instance, the Burgess Books of ports like Bristol and Southampton contain details of the apprenticeship bindings of sons of planters, giving their parentage and addresses overseas. If a person died abroad and left an estate in this country his will would have to be proved here, and it is worth looking at the indices of wills proved in the Prerogative Court of Canterbury for such entries. West Indian archives are also reasonably good and include wills and land grants as well as parish registers and gravestone inscriptions. Some of these archives have been copied and printed, and the list below includes some books which will help in tracing people of British descent resident in the West Indies. Mostly, though, you will need to write to the Archivist on the island concerned to find out what records he has in his care which may be of help to you.

Book List
Directory of British Associations 1977–8
J. Cox and T. Padfield   *Tracing your Ancestors in the Public Record Office* 1981
C. Barnett   *Britain and Her Army 1509–1970* 1970
C. Lloyd   *The British Seaman, 1200–1860* 1968
J.C. Hotten   *Original Lists of Persons Emigrating to America 1600–1700* 1874
G.F.T. Sherwood   *American Colonists in English Records* 2 volumes, 1932–3, 1969
P.W. Filby and M.K. Meyer   *Passenger and Immigration Lists Index* 3 volumes 1981
H.F. Waters   *Genealogical Gleanings in England* 2 volumes 1969
T. Wilkinson   *Two Monsoons: The British in India* 1976
V.L. Oliver   *Caribbeana* 6 volumes 1909–1919
J.H. Lawrence-Archer   *Monumental Inscriptions of the British West Indies* 1875
P. Wright   *Monumental Inscriptions of Jamaica* 1966

CHAPTER NINE
Writing A Family History

SOONER OR LATER you will want to decide how best to use the information you have gathered.

If you wish to produce an account of your family's history, you can either begin with yourself and trace your family back, or start with your earliest known ancestor and work forwards to the present day, but it is easier to add to your account if you begin with yourself. You can include a description of the distribution of your surname over the country or county, with suggestions as to its place of origin. Telephone Directories and a good book on surnames (see the booklist at the end of this chapter) will help.

You also need to decide whether you are going to write about your direct ancestors only or other branches of the family as well. If you include the other branches you should illustrate the text with pedigree charts of each branch, to avoid confusion in identifying members of your remoter family.

A much more entertaining approach is to describe your adventures as you searched, including photographs of relatives and places to break up the account. These may be copies of old family photographs, and photographs of street scenes, the houses where your family lived, the churches where they worshipped, and the gravestones commemorating those who have died. Include photographs of living relatives, named and dated, for they too will be ancestors one day. Always say where you saw the photographs and identify the people in them.

If you have original documents or copies, place them between polythene leaves, obtainable from most stationers' shops. You can then move them around easily, and their surfaces are protected from wear. The leaves can be inserted into an album, with labels to say what the documents illustrate and where they come from, and you can add a linking commentary.

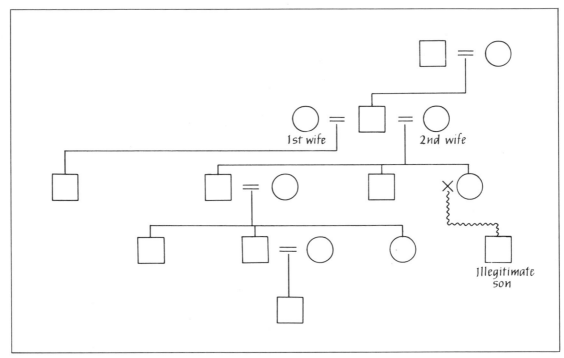

41   *A pedigree chart showing how to display an ancestor's first and second marriages with their issue, and how to indicate illegitimacy (with a cross and wavy line)*

You may like to send relatives who have helped you with information a copy of your story, or at least a copy of the pedigree chart; even at this stage you may find that someone can add extra information to it. Photocopying is cheaper than time spent making a handwritten copy which may contain mistakes.

If you want to meet other people in your area who are interested in family history, ask at the library or County Record Office for the address of the local Family History Society. The Secretary of the Federation of Family History Societies will also have a list of member Societies throughout the country and overseas. The Societies normally meet regularly for talks and practical evenings, and organize projects such as copying down gravestone inscriptions. Most of them publish a journal in which you can advertise your interest in a particular surname to other members. Obviously, if your family came from another part of the country it is best to join that Society or at least to place an advertisement in its journal.

The main Society in the United Kingdom is the Society of Genealogists, founded in 1911. Its library contains printed and original material unrivalled anywhere else, some of which I have mentioned in this book. You can pay a search fee to use its collections, or apply to join the Society.

By belonging to a Family History Society you can share in the interest of hunting for ancestors, just as you can pass down to your descendants something of your family's earlier history in your written account. Genealogy can give you a lifetime of pleasure as you try to unravel the past and piece together your personal heritage.

Book List
P.T.R. Palgrave-Moore   *How to Record Your Family Tree* 1979
W.P.W. Phillimore   *How to Write the History of a Family* 1887
D.J. Steel and L. Taylor   *Family History in Schools* 1973
H.B. Guppy   *The Homes of Family Names in Great Britain* 1968

Addresses

Public Record Office, Chancery Lane, London WC2A 1LR
Public Record Office, Census Section, Portugal Street, London WC2
Public Record Office, Ruskin Avenue, Kew, Richmond, Surrey TW9 4DV
General Register Office, St. Catherine's House, 10 Kingsway, London WC2B 6JB
Office of Population Censuses and Surveys, St. Catherine's House,
    10 Kingsway, London WC2B 6JB
Principal Probate Registry, Somerset House, Strand, London WC2R 1LP
British Library, Great Russell Street, London WC1B 3DG
Colindale Newspaper Library, Colindale Avenue, London NW9
College of Arms, Queen Victoria Street, London EC4V 4BT
House of Lords Record Office, House of Lords, London SW1A 0PW
Guildhall Library, Aldermanbury, London EC2P 2EJ
Historical Manuscripts Commission, Quality House, Quality Court,
    Chancery Lane, London WC2
India Office Library and Records, Foreign and Commonwealth Office,
    197 Blackfriars Road, London SE1 8NG
National Library of Wales, Aberystwyth, Dyfed SY23 3BU
General Register Office, New Register House, Edinburgh EH1 3YT
Court of the Lord Lyon, New Register House, Edinburgh EH1 3YT
Public Record Office of Northern Ireland, 66 Balmoral Avenue, Belfast BT9 6NY
General Register Office, 49–55 Chichester Street, Belfast BT1 4HL
Public Record Office, Four Courts, Dublin 7
General Register Office, Custom House, Dublin 1
Genealogical Office, Dublin Castle, Dublin
The Secretary of the Federation of Family History Societies,
    96 Beaumont Street, Milehouse, Plymouth PL2 3AQ
Society of Genealogists, 14–15 Charterhouse Buildings, London EC1M 7BA
The Institute of Heraldic and Genealogical Studies, Northgate, Canterbury
The addresses of other national ecclesiastical and local libraries and record offices
    may be found in *Record Repositories in Great Britain* 1982

Index